Party...

...Kim Einhorn

Party...

This book and my love is dedicated to Joanna and Max Jamilly.

Party... is also dedicated to David, my best friend and co-founder of Theme Traders. Without him, none of this would have been possible. Nor would 'Pod' the charity he founded 28 years ago exist. Starting with a party on the wards at Great Ormond Street Hospital for sick children, Pod was formed with the intent of bringing smiles to the faces of the many sick children. It currently holds over 1700 parties a year for children in hospitals and hospices. Well done DJ.

Party on... This is dedicated to Michel - a true party animal - and my lovely husband.

Contents

Introduction

Party ideas are two a penny...
...Making them happen is something else.

This book is meant for fun and as an ideas platform for any special occasions that you are planning...

It takes you through the fun and pitfalls of organising a great party the tittle tattle, and real life party stories and anecdotes...

Like Cookery books from around the world that are widely read and used for inspiration and recipes, Party... will complement every event and inspire you to create superb memorable talking points at your function. You can easily add that extra buzz, whether it is an intimate small dinner for two, a 21st birthday party or a large corporate event you will be able to take away ideas from Party... and use them on every level. From the design of the invitations, to the right cocktails for the theme; concepts for performers and music, ideas for catering and theming, let your imagination turn into reality. Included are over a hundred ideas and designs for popular themes, unique and amazing celebrations from around the world, and specialities of countries. These can all create ice-breakers and talking points, but more so, it will make each occasion more interesting and add sparkle to your event.

There have also been a lot of fabulous contributions from well known personalities, including celebrities, and designers, all of which answered the following party questions.

I hope that you enjoy their answers:

Which was the best party you have ever been to?

What made you enjoy it so much?

What was the wow factor?

If you had a dream party what would it be?

Party Planning Info

Party Planning Info

Putting together any event can be daunting as the further you get into the planning procedure the more you realize the challenges to be met.

As you are out to make it a great party you should also make sure you enjoy the party planning aspect. The way to assure everything goes smoothly is to actually have knowledge about the many varying aspects of the event and the challenges that go with it.

Consider which questions to ask suppliers and what aspects you want to organise yourself, or get the planner or contractor to do.

Think about the entertainment and music, performers and timings. Consider the design for the party and the style of food, canapes, buffet or silver service; will you simply hire the props and do the set up yourself? Or maybe you will decide to get in a professional party planner to organise the whole event or only the bits you do not like!

This chapter takes into account most of the questions and answers needed to tackle all the elements of your event. Make sure it is fun.

This is also the chapter containing true event stories and anecdotes demonstrating slight 'hiccupps' at parties!

The lovely memories of wonderful events experienced by our contributors really shines through.....

Atmosphere

The most important factor in realising the wow factor. This sets the scene for the event. Make sure you create this in some way, consider flame lights at the entrance to welcome your guests, sets of huge stilted creatures blowing bubbles from above, a UV reflective stunning entrance tunnel, something to capture the guests imagination when they arrive, something to wow them.

Atmosphere does not only mean the dressings, it can mean the touching of the senses at the event. Use perfume sprayed in the air, fresh flowers, smoke machines, sensual music relating to the theme, for an underwater event the sound of gentle waves, for a Thai event try Buddhists chanting.

A transformation of the space alone can create an atmosphere; add to it fun, music and imagination and your event will be a guaranteed success.

As guests enter you will know if your event is amazing by the actual 'Wow' that they emit, it is truly incredible, a reaction that generally is not thought about and a word that realistic is derived from nowhere! These all add to the overall atmosphere, try and apply it to your whole event.

At one party we organised, the atmosphere was electric from the beginning. We had a very realistic tiger statue emerging from the front door, the amount of guests who thought it was real was astonishing and this, followed by deep jungle sounds, screaming chimps and a moody entrance through hanging ivy, Indiana Jones style, created the atmosphere for a wonderful event. Though this was in a private house the effective entrance gave the event an excitement before anyone had even had a drink....The event depicted in the picture had a great atmosphere with superb meet and greet characters greeting guests as they entered the ballroom through a themed walkway at the Grosvenor House.

Audiovisual

This can be very important at a party and can say a million words; at a barmitzvah it can show the life of the child, at an award ceremony it will show the potential winners.

The choice of companies is vast. Choose the company you use carefully, make sure they have up to date equipment, and remember that it is more advisable to use a company who owns the equipment rather than using someone who is bringing it in from an unknown source. Be prepared for technical problems and always make sure the company you choose has made allowances for a back up procedure should anything fail to work.

Live feeds are fun, a kind of Big Brother feeling, fly on the wall TV. They can be used throughout an event, a few years ago video walls were all the rage, now they are retro and still fun.

Sound checks are extremely important, whether your event is at home or at a venue, never forget them, the same applies to the lighting, see everything working and allow plenty of time for tweaking and changes or it can all go wrong and you will have no time for alterations.

At one Bollywood banquet we made lovely pink and purple furniture, in exact colours for the banquette seating and also matching table cloths. It turned out to be a huge waste of both time and money when the AV company came in and lit it all in green and blue hues, this was their remit from the end client who had said they wanted the room 'washed' in those colours; our furniture became washed too, it no longer had the same feel, the colour mix did not work. The event was due to begin within the hour and the lighting company was adamant that the client required this strength of lighting and they would not dim them. On this occasion we were powerless to do anything, and as the client was nowhere to be found the show went on without the light changes,

Backdrops

Fantastic on a stage and behind discos and bands, star cloths also make great backdrops, often used at award ceremonies and to transform a whole room or area.

If themed backdrops are used behind food stations they work to enhance the style of the food that you are serving, for example an African food station would have statues, drums, tusks etc and would be very visible and distinct, against a safari background. Guests would also expect a particular type of food from it, as they would if the next station was set up as an American diner with a New York backdrop, and a third with a Pagoda and Oriental garden backdrop.

Backdrops can be hand painted or digitally printed from images to any size, and any colour. A nice touch is to arrange a customized backdrop to include some of your guests, family or theme.

Party Moments

Nigel Havers - Actor

My favourite party ever was my daughter Kate's 21st. The reason I enjoyed it so much was because it was a wonderfully happy night with all our friends. Kate looked radiant and I was so proud of her. We held it at home in Wiltshire in a marquee which was decorated very simply but with locally grown flowers and greenery from the garden.

I used to be in a band years ago and we re-formed for one night only to do a set for the ageing rockers before the real hard core disco began!! The clearing up was hell but I will never forget the happiness we all shared - it was really special If I could have that night all over again it would be my dream party - maybe with Marilyn Monroe thrown in just for me!

Balloons

One tip only – do not do them yourself unless you really know how or if they are for a children's party. Balloons can look magnificent if done professionally, if not, a simple disaster and childish.

Using colours such as gold and black stars on tables set on Hollywood style table centre looks great, so do wonderful hot air balloons 3ft in diameter set with a basket below filled with goodies for guests to take, it's fun and original. General balloon décor is great for low budgets as it can create a 'different view' for the party and does not cost much. Keep the balloon decorations uniform, though varying heights within a foot looks nice on the tables.

Remember balloons look sad very quickly, so make sure they are blown up at the latest time possible. Balloons say Party... and these silver ones attended a Pop Art party - Andy Warhol style.

Party Moments

Plum Sykes Socialite and Author

The best party I went to recently was the Met ball in New York. It was brilliant because they had flown in 7000 gardenias from all over the world, and the place smelled and looked incredible. Anna Wintour really knows how to throw a chic glamorous party.

My favorite thing was being there with my fiance Toby Rowland and one of my best friends Miranda Brooks. I have attended this party every year for the last seven years with miranda and its our girly tradition! My dress was Alexander Mcqueen, and it is **one of the** most incredible dresses I have ever gotten to wear.

Bands

Decide the music that you want and what it is to achieve.

A cover band is great for after dinner especially if there is a theme such as seventies then you could get a Blues Brothers style, band or perhaps for the 60s when you could use a Beatles Cover Band. There are some superb bands covering all different eras and styles of popular music which is great when everyone wants to dance, but totally inappropriate for a city cocktail party where the purpose is to network.

There is a huge range of bands out there, go and listen to them, or at least get a cd from them. If you have the budget you can always get a well known band, or singer. The same applies to jazz, soul, reggae and blues bands, all need to be briefed clearly.

In general musicians will not want to do sets longer than forty five minutes and then they will want to have a break. Normally they will do two sets or maybe one longer one. Make sure you know exactly what they will do and arrange their timing accordingly to get maximum impact.

Many singers often tend to have their own backing band and sound engineers but always check at the beginning what they are providing in the price, or budgets may be massively affected.

The sound system is of the utmost importance and you may find the band will have written into their contract exact specifications to meet. Make sure they have sound checks and the sound system is loud enough for the amount of guests you have.

Some bands are demanding, at one event we had to get champagne for them, even though wine was available, or they said they would not play, we had obviously missed that bit of the contract!

Banquets

An exciting word, creating a fantasy world of luxury and opulence.

Make it happen, wow your guests, huge candelabras in the centre of tables clad in velvets, massive urns filled with fresh fruits tumbling out onto the golden coloured damask runners, pewter goblets and pewter plates, all in a room dressed in the elegance of bygone days, grand 7ft candelabras with huge church candles, add wandering minstrels, jesters, and use long tables instead of rounds and you have a superb Medieval banquet.

When organising a banquet on long tables and with benches always make sure guests are ready to eat at the same time or there is a constant disturbance with people having to get up to let others sit!

Party Moments

Molly McKellar - PR Consultant

The best party I've ever been to was the last night Panto-On-Ice show at Wembly, which marked the end of my showbiz career.

I enjoyed it so much because, though decades ago, it is still memorable, packed with emotion... laughter and tears... all pledging to stay in touch forever.

The "WOW" factor was that everyone felt it was just for them. Individual gifts and photographs; wacky entertainment.

My dream party would be held in The Winter Palace at St. Petersburg with my favourite friends, plus Catherine the Great; Diaghilev; Nijinsky and Nureyev.

Bars

Ice bars, sleek bars, modern bars, pub bars, round bars, bamboo bars, the variety is endless. Go for the one that will enhance your event. If it is a large space themed event use a huge circular bar with an 8ft rocket in the centre, if it is a cool cocktail style party, Sex in the City, sleek curved chrome bars say it all. The bar should always be a talking point and can become the social point for the evening.

Is the function of the bar for getting drinks from? or a place where guests can hang around and chat? Do you need bar stools? a white fluffy bar with white fluffy stools and a big pink *I LOVE YOU* neon sign will certainly attract a lot of attention, add some special lighting effects and you have a great focal point. For fun you can have waiters going around with a pack strapped to their back to top up drinks, quite quirky really. Ice bars are trendy, but remember they tend to melt...

Party Moments

Jonathan Goldberg - Q.C.

My cousins wedding in Caesara in 2003 was the best party I ever attended.

There was a magnificent spectacle of entertainers, dancing and brilliant food in a beautiful garden on a warm spring evening.

The wow factor of the night were fire-eaters, jugglers and fiddlers on the roof.

My absolute dream of a party would be a cocktail party held in a roman amphi theatre with an opera performance to entertain my guests.

Be A Guest At Your Own Party

This has always been our motto and good organisation and planning can make it happen. Be dressed and ready two hours in advance, have a glass of champagne, walk around admire the décor and food and really relax.

During the event there is no doubt that you will enjoy yourself more if you are not worrying the whole time about the general running of the party, as clearly was shown in the following example at an event we worked at. It all took place in beautiful castle belonging to a Lord, there was an incident where the weather was so much warmer than expected that the magnificent ice bar started to melt at an alarmingly rapid pace, without the client being aware, during dinner, we quickly removed the bar and created another with an ice effect from fabric. The floor got mopped and the host and guests were none the wiser and very impressed by the lovely change in decor!

Other ways of assuring you really are a guest at your own party is to organise everything in advance have a very detailed checklist, timetable and to do list all the way through the organisation stages. Make sure you are very thorough about details, constantly update your lists and keep all the papers together in a file for quick reference, alternatively simply get in a party planner to oversee the whole event. This will add to the budget but is worth every penny if they are experienced, and without exception it is more valuable for you to have time to entertain your guests or network rather than worrying about things that may not be happening or are going wrong!

It does not matter which design you choose or how big the party is, from an intimate beautifully styled chilled out event for four guests to a grand occasion it is certainly going to be more fun for you and your guests if you have time to circulate and talk to them.

Party Moments

Isabel Losada - Author of the Battersea Road to Enlightenment and For Tibet with Love

I don't know about the best but I can tell you that my favourite party ever is one that I gave myself for a limited number of my friends. What made it so special was that I had asked a friend of mine who is a wonderful cook to do a 'Babette's Feast' style feast and she produced a spread that everyone wanted to photograph.

I don't like recorded music at parties and I had another good friend who is a wonderful pianist and can play anything in any key come and play my piano and I had another friend who is an illusionist amongst the guest and I loved seeing my friends gasp in amazement at his tricks.

It was the subtle delight of knowing that I had created a really great evening for a bunch of people that I'm fond of and the joy of seeing them meeting each other. I hold a large birthday party every year and some of them only ever meet at my parties. I love introducing people to each other.

Just the joy of seeing my friends have a great evening and possibly one of my friend's faces as she watched the illusionist bang a nine inch nail into his nose.

I would like to take all the people that I love for one reason or another (we are talking hundreds of people) to a tropical island for a couple of weeks all expenses paid. Then I could watch everyone having a good time for weeks.

Bouncers and Security Staff

They are the eyes and ears of the party, they take the strain away from you, unwanted guests are sent packing, and you can enjoy your party in comfort. Even one can make all the difference.

Celebrity events are always swooning with them, fortunately Bouncers tend to be good looking, have nice fit bodies and wear mostly black so they fit in nicely. Always brief them early and make sure they know where to contact the person in charge of any problems and who they are.

When you are having the party organised professionally, and if a batch of celebrities are attending or maybe if there are VIPs, it should become part of the brief of the party planner to deal with any incidents, leaving you to party in comfort. Walkie Talkies and Radios are a must for fast contact.

Party Moments

Ken Hom – Oriental Celebrity chef

My dream party was one that I put together myself. It was New Years Eve for 2000!
I enjoyed it immensely as I was the dj and I had everyone dancing until 7 in the morning!
My own pick of music really added the WOW factor.
At my own dream party, I would dj and would be supplied with lots of good wine to keep me going!

Budgets

Budgets are the guiding light for the party. You need to know from the start the level of money that you want to spend on your event, bearing in mind that it can be used simply as a starting point it will ease the way forward much faster and in a focused manner.

Usually, the first question that party planners get asked is 'how much will it cost' followed by 'please give me ideas for three different options,' ideas which are often thousands of pounds apart. This task is very time wasting for an event planner as you are asking them to do three times the amount of work when in reality, you are in control of the budget and generally know the levels that you are comfortable with. This applies to any event; set the budget in advance so you do not have to cut back later on things that you may have set your heart on and you feel are very important.

Budgetary guidelines need to be split carefully to accommodate all requirements, for example the choice of using an existing barn for a party or having a marquee can mean the difference of thousands of pounds. Always get an idea of the break down costs of the main elements in advance.

If you are simply having a party at home knowing the sort of budget you want to spend will help you plan the party more successfully from the beginning. It will no longer be a hit and miss situation where you may have a bit left for decorations and a disco but you are not really sure, and then you may end up not being able to get any of your first choices as you left it all too late to book.

From experience, clients tend to worry that the party planner will spend all the budget regardless, but what you are really asking them to do is to make a very special event on a level that you are comfortable with, and every time you cut back you will end up disappointed because something will have to go, so it is always better to begin from a realistic starting point.

Buffets

Buffets should be spectacularly laid out and if possible themed to the party. If it is a Western event, think about using a chuck wagon to serve from or as a centre point to the buffet. Serve from gondolas for Masked balls and Italian events. Use rustic barrels and wooden boards as counters for cheese at Irish and Cockney events. Use shipwrecked boats for fish dishes and nautical themes, ivy clad carts for fruit, coster monger barrows for meat dishes. Use themed backdrops behind the buffet, and dress up the catering staff to match the style chosen.

If the buffet has no theme and you want to lay the food out before the guests arrive, you can create a stunning looking design with simple twinkling lights and glowing cubes set in glasses, use these elements on the food table, the guests will take the glasses first and the food will still look glorious, magical and very special, keep the lights dim and play some powerful classical music.

Most of all the food must look appealing, no half empty dishes on the buffet, keep them topped up or put in a smaller dish, no scrappy bits all over the buffet. Most people eat first with their eyes, so enhancing the décor around the buffet really pays off. A styled and themed buffet should be used as one of the main focal points of a room.

Make sure, if you have a lot of guests, that you have several separate buffet points and there is no possibility you will end up with one boring long queue!

At a buffet the seating and handling of the food must also be looked at carefully. Where are the guests going to eat it? Should it be part seating or full seating? Should the food be finger food style or a full meal? Are the place settings laid at the table or are the guests going to have to get their own plates and cutlery? If so place them somewhere it is easy to see! It is extremely irritating to go to your table and find no cutlery or serviettes.

Caterers

There are only a few excellent caterers that have stayed the course; many like restaurants go in and out of fashion. The most well known companies which work at the exclusive events are more expensive for one reason only and that is because they are the best and give 150%. Bearing in mind you receive this extra attention to detail, perhaps they are not the most expensive at all, but are the ones who have allowed for highest quality and impeccable service. The best caterers do not tend to be part of large catering groups, instead they generally are passionate individuals or partners that have built a reputation for good food and offer a personal service.

Make sure you visit your caterer for a tasting, and to check out the presentation. If the food is fabulous but the presentation not, be wary as the caterer is normally also in charge of the serving staff, china, glasses and cutlery on the night and will probably not get that right either!

Recommendations for caterers are great, from trusted sources, but a cheaper alternative is to go to a catering agency and hire in the chef and serving staff yourself. This is more useful for smaller low budget parties and especially if you want to be involved in the preparation yourself.

Many restaurants now have outside catering facilities and offer this to their clients, and depending on budget it can work out very well. A friend of mine used a local Thai restaurant for a buffet for his fiftieth birthday party at home, they were incredibly kind and bent over backwards to help and they provided wonderful food at the low restaurant prices. At his next event when he had to feed two hundred international guests on a low budget he asked an Indian caterer, an ex national hockey champion, who had the concession in his sports club to undertake the event. It was held in a town hall, he brought in his friends to help with the service, all much cheaper than a normal external caterer and they were still covered by health and safety and food hygiene standards. All the catering turned out to be very tasty and once again through his resourcefulness very reasonably priced.

Champagne

Always a wonderful welcome and gratefully received by guests. Make sure you know which champagne you are serving, and always taste it first. Sometimes it is better to use sparkling wine, as some cheap champagnes are truly awful. Do bear in mind that there is a vast range of other lovely sparkling wines available that can be used instead of champagne if budget or taste is an issue.

When you serve Bucks Fizz there is very little point going for very expensive Champagne as it will become partially diluted. Always use freshly squeezed juices for all Champagne drinks.

Classic Champagne cocktails are fantastic yet, over the years the brandy has been exchanged for cointreau, like everything else fashion counts; fortunately the angostura and sugar have still stood the test of time!

At one event we worked at, though we were not in charge of the catering I must add, the client had specified that only Cristal champagne was to be used. She was very upset when it was brought out by the catering staff in glasses on trays for her guests with no bottles in sight, she felt the caterer had not understood that she wanted to give her guests more than just a glass of Champagne, but something very special.

Champagne is great after dessert for speeches especially at birthdays and weddings. An interesting way to serve it is to have an ice bucket with the Champagne and Champagne glasses set into it.

Champagne glasses come in many shapes and designs, wide brimmed ones are called Champagne saucers, very 1930s, and fabulous if you are having a matching champagne fountain. Fashionable nowadays are elegant hollow stemmed fluted glasses, where the champagne flows to the very bottom. There is also of course the classical cut glass stemmed Champagne flute, which is simply beautiful.

Chill Out Areas

So fashionable these days are modern sofas, low tables, and mixed sizes of soft cushions all colour co-ordinated to the event, and set in small intimate areas. You do not need extensive seating, just an area for some guests to relax and chill after dinner. These should be attractive little areas, use pretty t-lights on the tables and have low-level lighting.

Think about having an entertainer of some sort wandering around. Magicians, Caricaturists, or Tarot readers all work well. Create the areas away from the dance floor and near to the bar

It also looks great to create further intimacy by having some beaded curtains or drapes pulled back around the area. At themed parties add props for fun, try a surfboard for an Aussie theme, and maybe bubbling columns colour matched to the area for any scheme.

Party Moments

Bruce Oldfield - Designer

The best party was a party I hosted for Krug champagne to celebrate 40 years of Henri Krug at the helm. It was held at Syon House and the 60 guests drawn from the arts mainly were treated to a lavish dinner on a 40ft table, drinking fine champagnes with every course.

I enjoyed it because it felt like I was given dinner at home, it was relaxed and cosy in spite of being in the palatial surroundings of Syon House - which was it's WOW factor.

Clean Up

If it is a large party make sure you arrange with your party planner prior to your event to organise cleaners or remember to get in specialist cleaners yourself to organise the clean up.

Arrange for the cleaners to arrive late as you will be tired the following day. Try and go out while they are working! Nothing like coming back to a house that has been cleaned by fairies.

If you are having the event at home inevitably there will be spilt drinks, carpet cleaning, polishing, washing and general wear and tear after any party. There is nothing worse than spending the next few days sorting out the mess.

If you are cleaning it yourself - good luck!

Party Moments

Jerry Hall - Model and Actress

The best party I have ever been to was my birthday.

I enjoyed it very much as it was my birthday.

The presents were the WOW factor and if I were to have a dream party, it would be my next birthday!

Cocktails

Cocktails always go down a treat, especially if served by a Tom Cruise style bar man...

If used correctly cocktails really add to your theme and give off many messages, for Beach parties, try tropical rum cocktails. Chic and stylish go with James Bond, Martinis stirred and not shaken..

Be aware that you may book a 'cocktail barman' and be expecting him to throw the bottles around, he may drop them if he tries! If you want a barman that is an entertainer as well, make sure you check out he can juggle bottles, as having a cocktail barman only really means he knows how to make the cocktails correctly!

Using a slush puppy machine for Marguerites is a great idea for Summer parties.

Party Moments

Alan Titchmarsh - Gardening Expert and Novelist

My own 50th birthday was a dream party.
I had no knowledge of it and so no worries about the planning!
The great thing was that I was so in the dark about it and that all my real friends were there.
My dream party would consist of my closest friends- no more than 50 of them, here at home in our barn with food and drink and jolly old-fashioned dancing. Fab!

Party Moments

Bolette Peterson - Horse whisperer, breeder of racing horses and Horse healer

The best party I have ever been to was Sheikh Mohammed Al Maktoum's 'Desert Party' in Dubai, about 8 years ago. It was the first time he did this party, so it was exclusive and very exciting and new It was during the Dubai World Cup week, and everyone in Racing was in town for the festivities. I was staying with a friend who trains horses in Dubai, so he had organised everything for me. We all went on buses through the desert to a secret destination, and as we approached the party site we were astounded by the huge white tents in the horizon, in the middle of nowhere. Flares lit our approach along the sandy path after leaving the buses, and an air of excitement and intrigue surrounded the event. We had no idea what we were in for!

Stalls of local produce lined the path, and we were welcome to help ourselves to anything. Champagne flowed as we walked into a huge square, tents lined all around the square, like Bedouin tents, with exotic carpets and pillows surrounding lavish tables for our feast. The main racing people were there so I was surrounded by many friends, which definitely added to the party atmosphere, and everyone was excited. There were belly dancers, fire eaters, people walking around on stilts, traditional dancers, music, and food from all over the world. The party went on all night and the extravagance was unlimited! The evening finished with the most incredible fireworks I had ever seen in my life…unforgettable!

I enjoyed the evening so much because I was surrounded by friends in a totally different place to normal. Usually I see them racing and at various horse auctions, so to be in a situation like that was such a treat. Also the surprise element, not knowing where we were going and what we were going to, really did it for me!

Sheikh Mohammed didn't miss a thing, he had thought of everything and everything was provided for. I think he knew that the tents in the desert would amaze everyone, and it did, it certainly took us by surprise.

And…if I had all the money in the world! I would have a party beside Lake Maggiore in Italy. A huge dance floor with floodlights and wispy smoke around the edges with the lake in the background. A few rowing boats tied to the side so people can row out onto the lake in the moonlight. Everyone would be dressed in the finest black tie and the location would be secret. They would all be picked up from their hotels in limos, and have their eyes covered so the element of surprise would heighten the excitement.

Upon their arrival to the party, they would be greeted by a display of white dancing horses, and they would perform for them as they entered the venue. Tables with beautiful displays would be scattered around for the finest supper. During supper the guests will be entertained by a chorus of a top west end performance, before heading onto the dance floor out by the lake.

Gifts would be given to all the guests so that they would never forget their evening!

Dance Floor

These can be dressed in any style. If, for example you surround any dance floor with a balustrade, add urns and stunning floral arrangements and it lends itself to summer parties, weddings, sheer radiates elegance and generally just looks lovely, consider using a stone effect dance floor to complement it.

Dance floors come in all shapes and sizes. They can be totally transformed to fit the atmosphere, theme and decor. We created a Union Jack in Italian colours for an Italian launch, a truly stunning dance floor. A silver dance floor looks great for a futuristic party, a multi coloured dance floor for the seventies and Saturday Night Fever Disco style events, black and white dance floors for Blues Brothers, add fabulous lights moving or static and the mood changes again. Marbled dance floors are beautiful for Titanic, and thirties events where decadence was the name of the game.

At one event we logoed the client's crest in silver to the centre and it looked amazing.

Flashing dance floors are wonderful for cool events, and so are floors set with tiny lights.

Traditional dance floors usually come in wooden parquet, which is OK for most events and used extensively by hotels. They tend to be the cheapest style of dance floor available. If you are having a Western party surround it with hay bales and coral fencing,

Dance floors also come, as standard in black and white which looks very smart and stylish for any party, and even the beautiful marbled dance floors, are now easily available.

The size of the dance floor should reflect the amount of guests you are having, it is better to have a smaller dance floor as people enjoy the intimacy more than rattling around on an oversized one.

Dancing

Everyone loves dancing, whether it is to a disco, a band, a jukebox or sound system, after a few drinks their foot starts tapping.

It is generally best to start the dancing after the meal. A good and easy way of encouraging guests onto the dance floor is by introducing a small dance act and encouraging participation, especially where you have introduced a theme, for a 1950s Rock and Roll party an exhibition Jive troupe can create a fast moving show and then the dancers can go and get guests to dance with them, this never fails. Another great dance act is the Moulin Rouge style Can Can girls, they always find guys willing to participate especially when they are wearing their gorgeous corsetted costumes! Line dancing is fun at a hoe down; and everyone loves dancing to the rhythmic Reggae beat of Bob Marley. It is also possible now to have a silent disco - a brilliant spectacle.

When you arrange the music for dancing make sure you have indicated the tempo and style, there is nothing worse than the wrong type of music at the wrong times and for the wrong event.

As a rule of thumb start the dance music fast and end the evening with slow dancing.

It is a good idea to organise a dance play list in advance for the event. If it is for example a wedding, favourite tunes can be digitally recorded in advance in a set order to create continuity after the speeches when the bride and groom start the dancing, this can also apply to most other occasions.

Keep an eye on the mood of the guests and the music playing or you may end up with a deserted dance floor. You can always rely on a good DJ to cover that aspect

Remember to wear comfortable shoes if you are going to dance all night...

Decorations

Decorations are a must, regardless of how you decide to use them.

They say you have made an effort for your guests. Simple elements such as a wonderful huge prop may become the talking point for the evening, for example a Marilyn Monroe statue, especially the classic one with her skirt blown up, will get a lot of comments all evening. Small decorations to the food, beautiful floral arrangements and special touches all mean a lot.

If you decided to set Marilyn as the focal point and then to theme further you could include neon's, off white table cloths, clapperboards with her movies on, and if you really want fun, organise some giveaways, perhaps blonde Marilyn wigs for the guests, believe me they will all wear them! That will also provide you with great amusing photo memories of guests having fun at your party.

At a slightly more formal event a statue such as a Henry Moore abstract style can be lit with changing mood lighting. This alone creates a talking point.

Decorations look wonderful, if budget allows get them done by a specialist theming company, if not simply hire them directly from the same company and install them yourself.

At Theme Traders we have over three thousand images of decorations and all available on line, this makes it very easy to choose a scheme. Putting together a whole scheme is a very skilful job, yet very easily accessible for anyone who wants to have a go and design their own style of event.

Do bear in mind that if you decide to hire only it takes creativity and time to set up party decorations. If at all concerned, make sure you visit the prop hirers, view the props and let them chat you through all possibilities; this tends to be a free service when you hire from them and will be invaluable.

Design

Designing an event should be fun... You are creating a set, a live picture for you and your guests.

Every event requires design. Every thought that you put into the event is connected with the overall expectations you have for the party and the way you are planning to achieve it, this is design. A well designed party or event does not need to be crammed full of décor or theming it needs to be well thought out to reflect the image you wish to portray.

Pure white walls washed in pastel tones, white and pastel tablecloths, white-flecked orchids with scattered petals at their base, all suggest minimal, and reflect a particular style. Iconic props such as Tiffany lamps on small tables, deep red velvet curtains on the stage, chaise lounge, set alongside podium dancers all within a moody red tinted atmosphere, lend themselves to a boudoir design.

If you are designing the party yourself set it all on paper first, and then work out a plan and possible scheme bearing in mind budgetary constraints and your own creativity.

If you are using a party planner they will take a brief from you and then work with you on the design throughout with the design in mind. Visuals of the party design should also be available from the party planner, though these tend to be chargeable unless the party is confirmed. They are extremely important as it assures you that you are both interpreting the design in the same way and there will be no surprises.

Design is purely a matter of taste and nothing is right and nothing is wrong. There may be a purpose or message in the party design, if the guests can relate to it the event will have achieved success.

Having a well designed party is also a great key to unlocking the Wow factor.

Discos

Discos come in all shapes and sizes, with and without lighting, with or without decks, with or without rigs. Ensure you discuss in detail your requirements and book the right style of disco. A large event will need extra amplifiers and speakers as well as a great lighting rig whereas a smaller event may simply need a DJ, decks and speakers.

The structure can vary enormously depending on your requirements, the disco and sound desk can often be linked to the overall sound system for use during speeches. Make sure if this is the case, that you brief both the sound engineer if there is one, and also the DJ that you will need them to be available early on. They often disappear until their spot, and you do not need a sudden panic!

Remember there may be copyright issues with the music you play so check it out.

The style of DJ you choose also is relevant to the event, it not wise to get one who specialises in garage and hip hop if the age group requires a good all rounder with classical chart toppers. Always chat through the play lists in advance, it is now also very easy to choose exactly the songs you require for the whole evening and organise special songs dedicated to particular people.

Recently I organised my nieces sixteenth birthday party, I felt it was absolutely essential that the DJ needed to be flexible and in tune with young people. I also felt that he should be trendy and friendly, as the girls would really enjoy watching him and would be encouraged to dance. Sticking an old timer in there as a DJ was not appropriate for this age group regardless of how good he may be, unless of course he had celebrity status, maybe Robbie Williams. The DJ was a big hit and he allowed some of the young aspiring DJ guests to have a go on his decks, the whole event had a new and fun inter active talking point and activity, and of course all the girls ended up fancying him!

Drinks

Champagne, wine and water are great to offer guests as they come in, add cocktails to the tray if it is a themed party and it fits in, it will definitely start the ball rolling.

The choice of drinks and glasses makes a difference, theme them to your event. Red and black glasses for Fire and Ice, frosted white glasses for Winter Wonderland, over sized cocktail glasses with umbrellas for Carnival. Try serving Sangria with red glowing cubes for a Spanish party, tequila shots for Mexico, vodka for White Russia. Make every detail count.

If you are having a sit down meal the choice of wines is endless, some hosts carefully select a choice of different wines to accompany each course, generally this will have been advised by the chef and complement the food, others simply choose a good red and white and stick to them.

I would always advise a bottle and a half of wine per person, simply because guests would find it very hard to drink that much and you would not run short over a group of people.

You can always get sale or return from caterers and wine shops. There is nothing worse than running out of wine at a party. An amount of beer should also be available for those special guests who require it. Whenever possible it is nice to have available a fully stocked bar for aperitifs, cocktails and shorts.

Obviously each event has its own set of criteria and that will effect the drinks allowed throughout the party, a twenty first birthday party is much more suited to beer and wine, a cocktail party to champagne and sparkling wine, a carol concert lends itself to mulled wine, for a Beach party colourful cocktails can be sipped under the cool shade of a palm tree.

Entertainment

Comedians, dancers, magicians, fairground stalls, tattoo artists, caricaturists the list is endless, tailor it to your audience – your guests.

An opera scenario is not suitable for guys 21st birthday party with a Mods and Rockers theme; give him pretty podium dancers in sixties costumes. A comedian is not suitable for foreign guests, who would not understand the language enough to find the jokes funny, try a mime act instead. Steer away from stage acts if the audience is very diverse, as you will not please them all; try using fun games and roving performers, something for everyone.

Check out the performers prior to booking theme, or only get them on recommendations especially if they are inter-acting with the guests.

If you book entertainments directly make sure you see a copy of their public liability insurance. We arranged a circus workshop for a group of city people, a rather large lady decided to try and learn stilt walking, she put one foot on the stilts an elevation of six inches - lifted the other, came off and twisted her ankle, first she tried to sue the company she worked for as they had arranged the workshop, then she tried the conference organiser, then the production company -us- then finally the buck stopped with the poor guy who was helping her to learn, he ended up in court and then having his insurance premiums increase dramatically. She had wanted to gain financial reward for something she willingly participated in and wanted to do, the drop was the same as a street kerb. If the performer had not had liability insurance the whole thing would have become very messy.

If you have booked acts or entertainments through your party planner or an agent this should all be taken care of. They should have checked performers credentials, insurance, performing abilities and be happy to recommend them and use them on all of their events.

Entrance

Making sure that guests feel welcome at the entrance can make or break a party. Always be there to greet them, thank them for coming, they may well have brought a present for you, if there is time, open them, do not however start to create a queue!

The entrance should be looking lovely, unique and dramatic, maybe a modern blue lit tunnel with the drinks served at the end. Consider many fire beacons lighting up the drive, or a walk-through wardrobe Narnia Style. Match the music to the event design and ensure it is all exciting.

Make sure there is someone to look after coats, and offer your guests a drink immediately. Be prepared for latecomers, always have a few fresh bottles put away for them, there is nothing worse than wandering around trying to find the host and a drink when you arrive at a party.

Party Moments

Richard Young - Paparazzi Photographer

The best party I've ever been to was The Vanity Fair Oscar Night party in LA, I've been there for the past six years and each one gets better and better. Being in LA on Oscar night is amazing. The glamour, glitz, the ambiance, the work that goes into the party and the AAAAA list of stars who all like to be photographed!

Being in LA for a week is a real WOW, shopping, staying at the Beverley Hills Hotel, the hospitality Vanity Fair show and my wife being there.

My dream party would be to have everyone I've ever dreamed of photographing there, but have sadly passed away - Jean Harlow, Charlie Chaplin, Marilyn Monroe, Errol Flynn, and to have Bob Dylan doing the music.

Party Moments

GARY RHODES - Celebrity chef

The best party I have attended was at the Natural History Museum and all of the dinosaurs had been dressed in funky clothes and boots. Very funny and artistic. It was a great evening with good friends and we had a wonderful evening in a fantastic venue and with a superb atmosphere.

The wow factor was James Brown. No one had any idea at all that he was at the venue and it was kept a secret until the end when he came on stage and sang live - Absolutely amazing and something I will never forget.

My dream party would be a big live show with some of the funkiest musicians and bands around, including the star of the evening which, for me, would have to be Stevie Wonder. He would ideally be supported by people such as Usher, Snoop Dog & more...

The ultimate would be to have a little tap on the shoulder with a voice asking me if I'd like a soft, slow dance. I'd turn around and it would be Marilyn Monroe. I'm dreaming already!

Flooring

The flooring needs special consideration. Whether you are using a marquee, a venue or your house if budget allows co-ordinate the flooring colour to your design or theme.

Wooden floors look great for School Discos and also the steerage section at a Titanic party. Be adventurous, try a blue and white striped floor for a Naval theme, or emerald green astro turf to represent the Emerald city in The Wizard of Oz. Bright red carpet looks stunning at Christmas. A colourful shaggy carpet is fun for 70s and Austin Powers, while Arabian Nights lend themselves to intricate Persian rugs. Coconut matting is great for both Oriental and Caribbean parties.

At one Flight theme party we built a runway with tracks of runway lights leading to a horizon where the sun set during the evening, it was stunning. Guests entered through the custom built plane.

If you use a marquee you will definitely need flooring unless the marquee is put over flat ground and over a smooth dry surface. When you are using a marquee in summer, the idea of grass under foot is great, be aware of the weather though, you may end up with a damp soggy mess. Always make sure the marquee has had its floor covering laid properly, we recently attended an event to do the theming, the floor had been put down shoddily and did not reach the edges of the tent!

As a general rule black carpet always looks nice, do not get the dull grey or blue often offered by marquee companies, there is little difference in cost, but a huge difference in overall appearance.

If there are various rooms and areas you can quite easily use different colour carpets and flooring effects. Consider having special messages added on the carpet, or tyre tracks for a Formula One party, or even Tinkerbell's footprints.

Flowers

Stunningly arranged floral displays can be superb, especially if done by a great floral designer. Artistic use of flowers is way of creating beautiful decorations, adding colour, mood and scent all in one go

Always bring flowers in line with the ambience, do not use spring flowers for themed events such as Moulin Rouge, use white lilies, as they will fit in stunningly. For Easter however daffodils are beautiful, for Christmas use holly ivy and red berry nests and add huge church candles

Flowers can be used to add to, or create the style of the event, they all have distinct characters. Long-stemmed deep red roses are passionate and elegant, use these on the tables for dressing candelabras which are clad in velvets, white tulips cut evenly will look fresh and modern in a square vase.

Rose petals look lovely scattered at the bottom of table centres and mirror bases, Rhododendrons are powerful and create superb worldly displays when set in metal globes, birds of paradise say hot, colourful and tropical, add palm leaves and you have a wonderful colourful display, a single orchid plant set in an bamboo rice steamer looks fabulous as a table centre at a Chinese party.

You can be very adventurous with flowers, we set a model of a Mini car in the bottom of a vase, logoed the sides of the vase in reds and oranges with the word Mini, added three brightly coloured gerberas and ended up with a great table display for a Mini launch. It reflected both the car and the funky era the car was born in namely The Swinging Sixties.

Trellis covered in fabrics and flowers are ideal for separating and defining areas. Large displays on classic plinths flanking an entrance look spectacular.

Focal Points

How many, is the question? Well the answer must be whatever your budget and party design allows; it is better to concentrate on a few good ones than have a wishy-washy scheme throughout.

The entrance, stage and tables should be the number one focal points to consider for your event. General décor around the venue can add a huge amount but should be left alone if budget is very tight. Depending on the style of event creating the talking points may need to be less than subtle.

Product launches tend to fall into this category, companies will go to a lot of trouble to put their product on the market and will brand extensively throughout the event, usually matching it to their advertising campaign. Often it will include ongoing audiovisual coverage, oversized products, and photo opportunities against a backdrop of the product.

At one event we created a Matrix style low level laser ceiling in a very high room, this was truly a show stopper, guests entered through a silvery space tunnel to a disappearing never ending spectacle of colourful lasers, with smoke twirling and special effect sounds - it was certainly a memorable focal point, exciting and also a great talking point.

Visual displays will add to the ambience, a marquee with a see through side can be dressed internally with pulled back drapes, add dramatic lighting to the outside garden and that itself looks beautiful, add a few up lit classical statues and you have an amazing focal point.

Live statues are incredibly popular, scantily clad or dressed to match the event. We were involved in the grand opening of a new department store in Turkey and used live statues amongst the forty performers we provided. The statues stood in each department with fabulous surreal headwear and costume each representing a department, including handbags and oversized shoes!

Food Glorious Food

It must look gorgeous, be appetizing and taste delicious.

Always have alternatives for vegetarians, guests with religious principles and those with special diets. Consider carefully the alternatives, not everyone likes mushrooms!

Canapés at the reception are always nice, make sure that whoever is serving them knows what they are in advance as some guests are sure to ask. The better they look the faster they will disappear, and if they taste wonderful make sure you have plenty!

Serve food in unusual ways, out of martini glasses as The Fat Duck does; on a platter for an Elizabethan wedding, and from a Lazy Susan at an Oriental banquet, this all enhances the appetite.

The food needs to be well thought out, try to bring it into the style of the event, for a Russian party add a little caviar and give the course a Russian name, for British serve Beef Wellington.

Design and create lovely menus, they will get the palate working, bear in mind that lots of people are real foodies and they will not appreciate low quality food, always serve highest quality even if it means you serve less courses.

Be creative with the desserts, take into account the weather, the last thing you want is the food running all over the place, like ice cream on a very hot summers day, go for berries or summer fruits with cream instead. Always have a light option, and a plate of lovely chocolates never go amiss.

It really does not matter to guests what food you choose to serve as long as it is fresh, looks good and tastes great. Do however make it clear on the invite whether you are feeding them!

Games

Indoor fairground games are great fun and marvellous at all events and functions. They tend to come in bright fairground colours and can be themed to any event; coconut shies become pineapple shies when dressed with red and gold fabrics for South Pacific parties, rifle ranges become ghost shooting ranges at Halloween, by using black tattered cloths some dangling skeletons and ghostly targets all UV lit. Add sound effects and dress the performer running the game as a Vampire, and you have a customised game ideal for your theme.

Other games to consider are the oversized games such as giant Jenga, Connect Four and Twister; depending on the style of your event you can either hire them in or get your party planner to create an easy package for you including a costumed performer to run the games. Table games such as quizzes, auctions, and mind bender games are very good for participation and fun.

Stylised and customised games are terrific for interaction and also for fund raising at charity events, they create interest and amusement and can fit into any theme. At fun days they are valuable as both parents and children can participate together. Horse Racing games and Scalextric are also popular and can easily be used in conjunction with a theme. Like a Casino, these games give the guests an opportunity to gamble, though only with fun money.

At one of the launches we did for Iron Maiden, as well as transforming the halls into a stunning set, we created custom games and activities matched up to their new album. Each album track had a game for it, and the game was themed extensively, even to the point where one incorporated a confession chamber with a transvestite priest. He was very popular all night and the stories we heard about the confessions given by guests were astonishing! This whole event got immense coverage on MTV and a member of the band was quoted as saying he really did not know what was going on!

Gifts For Guests

A lovely idea and always welcomed.

These can be given as guests arrive, perhaps if you have an overall theme and the event is not fancy dress, a little gift that they can wear will make all the difference. Flower leis being presented by a hula girl in a stunning Tropical paradise setting, feather boas at a Prohibition party being given out by Mac The Knife, ten gallon hats and string ties at the Oil Barons Ball.

Gifts on tables are also very well received, at Christmas parties, for example party poppers and funny hats. At Masquerade balls try beautiful masks on sticks, these can be put in a vase and will double up as a beautiful centrepiece. Customised gifts are also a great souvenir, try miniature Baileys, Brighton Rock, and chocolate objects, they will all be well received as they are fun and tasty.

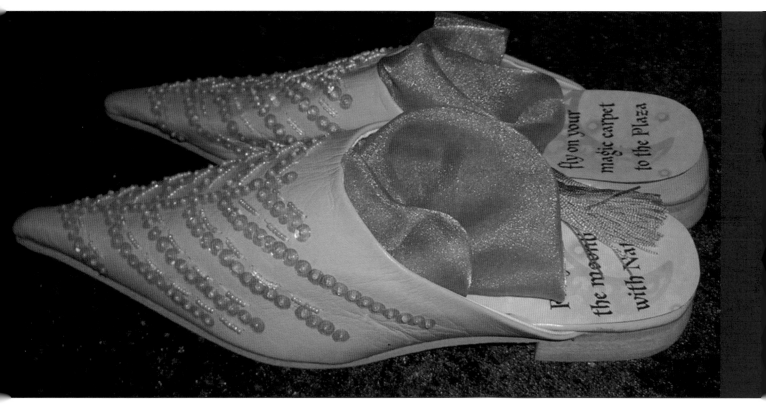

At corporate functions the directors often give presents, they may be expensive and are meant as a thank you to their employees. I attended one party where the company actually gave presents to the partners of their employees and thanked them for putting up with their partners while they worked so hard! They all received a small whiskey flask in silver. I am sure this did not make up for the divorce rate if the employees really were working a 14 hour day, everyday!

If you really want to make a big impression from the beginning you could send out a gift with the invitation, for an Indian party perhaps an incense box with a scroll invitation and joss sticks, for Lord of the Rings a small glowing ring with the ring around the invitation and a message to say 'entry only with the ring'. A party encompassing a Silk Trail theme could use a pair of ornate Turkish slippers, with all the details written on the shoes, once again these could be used as the pass to the party - and in the case of teenage gatecrashers it creates an easy identification system.

Health and Safety

Health and safety is the most important factor in any party you are organising. Bearing in mind that your guests may get a little tipsy every precaution must be taken in advance to prevent accidents.

Always have a first aid kit and important telephone numbers somewhere obvious. Unfortunately there is a trend to 'sue, sue, sue' which creates a huge strain on a party planner, as it is very rarely accidents happen because of their negligence and is generally more the case that the guest acted rather carelessly, for example trying to ride a rhino at 2am and then being surprised when asked to get off in case of a fall. The best bit of advice is not to use anything that may cause an accident, and ensure that there is someone in charge of health and safety throughout the event. This sounds easy but in reality how far can you go? At one event, a journalist went behind a barrier to avoid a queue, walked into a security guard who had his dog on the lead and got bitten. Negligence?

Party Moments

Jeannie Savage - Glamour Photographer

The Best party I've ever been to was Gary Cockerill's 30th bithday at The Hempel.

It was fabulous because there were lots of page three girls, people from the business and an excellent DJ.

The fact that we didn't have to pay for drinks was a real WOW factor!

If I were to have a dream party it would be at the Playboy mansion in Los Angeles!

Hiring

Anything at all can be hired for your party, a beautiful chateaux in France, an Aston Martin from the Bond movies, the Red Arrows, and even an ex-president of the United States.

Whatever your theme is, the possibilities are endless. You can get in a speciality theming company, who unlike regular hire companies will have a much fuller range of props to complement every aspect of the theme from the smallest detail; they will also be able to offer you a full custom, design and set up service. If you want the challenge, and are not put off by the lugging and immense work involved, you can hire in beautiful props and set them up yourself. These are the alternatives to using a party planner, event management company, or production company, who would organise all the above as part of their brief. Bear in mind that hiring may have extra costs involved, for example transportation for props and performers, and further fees if goods are returned late.

If you do use professionals, especially if your party is large scale a lot of the responsibility will be placed firmly in their hands, that is after all what they are being paid for. This means that you will not need to go to one place for backdrops and another for table centres, and another for stages another for costumes, you can use the company as a one-stop shop.

Always go and view the venue, and hire company to ensure you are comfortable with all the hired elements, if you do not have the time at least view their images on-line. In our image database we also put details of the prop sizes, quantities and weights, all very important, as both the organiser and end client need to know what they are really getting. Viewing an image database is great as an ideas tool at the preliminary stages of a party, and if the company has a showroom you should visit it, as you will certainly be inspired.

Party Moments

Mary Kay Eyerman - Journalist and Editor of The London and UK Datebook

After 15 years as a partner in a special events company in the States and then 12 years of involvement with a special events publication, I can honestly say that I have worked on or attended a great many functions. However, without a doubt, the most fantastic event I have ever attended was Liberty Weekend, July 1986 in New York City.

The actual event was on Friday but for us it started the night before with a cocktail reception and buffet dinner for committee members and special guests. Friday 4th July was one of those perfect summer days – not too hot, light breeze and plenty of sunshine. We boarded a private launch which took us to Governors Island for a continental breakfast prior to taking our place in the reviewing stand for the start of the program, which began with an International Naval Review - 21 foreign naval ships from 14 countries joined 11 US Navy vessels with President Ronald Regan aboard the U.S.S. Iowa.

The program included the Liberty Fanfare composed by Roger Williams; remarks by Lee Iacocca, Chairman of the Statue of Liberty -Ellis Island Foundation, and an address by Ronald Reagan, President of the United States. The morning's festivities concluded with Operation Sail'86 Parade of the Tall Ships. More than 265 sailing ships from over 30 countries cruised by the reviewing stand. It was absolutely incredible!

And there was more to come! A typical Fourth of July picnic lunch was served in a private tent before we returned to New York City. Once there, we had a choice of attending the Harbour Festival or an afternoon at leisure before once again joining the committee, special guests and President Reagan for cocktails and dinner.

And how does one end a day like this? With a fireworks spectacular of course! This was, up to this time, the country's biggest-ever fireworks display set off from a string of barges stretching around the Battery from the lower Hudson River to the East River - over five miles in length!

The entire day was absolutely spectacular! What was the 'WOW factor? This was a once in a lifetime, never to happen again, event. How special is that!

Each guest would be picked up in a chauffer driven Bentley with champagne in the car. They are driven nearest airport where guests board a private jet for a flight to Egypt. During the flight, caviar and champagne would flow as special entertainment is presented. Upon arrival in Egypt, guests would board a luxury coach for the drive to Abu Simbel where a buffet in front of the temple would be served. After the buffet there would be entertainment before boarding the coach to travel back to the private jet for the return trip where chauffeurs would be waiting to take the guests to their home.

Quick Note: Tom Eyerman was a member of the Statue of Liberty-Ellis Island Centennial Commission Advisory Panel.

Host's Role

This is quite simple, it is to look after your guests and make sure they have a great time.

The reason for the event is not relevant, whether it is for networking, socialising or celebrating, it is up to the host to ensure that the guests are well looked after. You can get help from a party planner who will recommend a series of ways to assure that your guests enjoy themselves. They will offer ideas, possibilities and diverse entertainments. Always try to have a way of entertaining all the ages, try using a table-to-table entertainer to amuse less mobile people, so they do not feel left out if all the youngsters are dancing and they can not, they will really appreciate it and you will have made them feel welcome from your consideration.

It is up to the host to make sure people talk to each other, build friendships and have fun

Party Moments

Jessica Taylor – Liberty X

My 24th birthday party I shared with Michelle was the best party I've ever been to.

Everyone I loved was there and there was an amazing atmosphere which made it very special.

The Wow factor was that it was made personal to me. The decoration looked amazing.

My dream party would include gorgeous men waiting on me! It would take place on a desert island, with good music, and all my friends around me.

Icebreakers

Little fun gifts, spectacular performers, celebrity look a likes, they can all amaze your guests, the WOW factor, wonderful food and wines, but most of all create inter- action with other guests,

Try meet and greet Paparazzi, snapping away and asking risqué questions to your guests as they arrive, down the red carpet, 'is it true that you are now seeing Liz Hurley and she's having your baby?' The answer invariably will be 'I wish' followed by laughter from everyone nearby.

Other icebreakers can be hugely amusing and imaginative, a ride on a sultan's chair to the venue for an Arabian nights event, a tug of war at a summer garden party, table football tournaments during the world cup. Unusual cocktails and brilliant cocktail barmen, vodka luges shaped in an erotic fashion, and even something like being asked to take your shoes off for a Geisha themed party.

Party Moments

Michelle Heaton - Liberty X

The best party I've ever been to was the party Sarah did for my birthday last year at Trap.

It was wonderful as all my friends and family were there and the music was great.

That it was made personal to me was a big WOW factor. I felt very special.

My dream party would be to Light up a beach at night, have a barbeque and a bonfire, with all my friends wearing beach wear, and live music playing.

Insurance

Rule number one - know which suppliers have got it and what it covers - get copies of insurance.

All the performers, caterers, entertainers should have their own public liability insurance as will the party planner; they will also have collated insurance documents from services they provide and sub contract in for the event. Consider taking out a single party insurance yourself to cover all possibilities. This is a wise idea and should cover all aspects of the event.

If you are having your event at a venue you will find they have a public liability insurance to cover them. Other companies that you employ should also have insurance covering their services. If they do not have insurance, do not use them, it is not worth the risk, and you may also find that the venue will not let them work there anyway.

There are many aspects of insurance elements to consider. If you are having valet parking be sure that there is insurance for the drivers. Be aware if guests get too drunk at a party the host can be sued if there is an accident.

At one golf club a lady arriving in her car got out and tripped on the pebble car parking, and she sued the golf club successfully, received compensation and they also had to take away the lovely pebbles from the car park and cover it in tarmac. This in my opinion was ridiculous and she should simply have been more careful, regardless of my opinion she still won her claim. I was recently interviewed for an article by the Guardian newspaper on just such a matter, they had information that many companies were not prepared to have events at Christmas because of the liability risk, My opinion was that party goers should be made responsible for their own actions and not claim unless it is really a case of negligence. The argument goes on throughout the industry, the premiums go up and the possibilities of having wild parties dwindle.

Invitations

These can take a variety of forms. They can be uniquely designed reflecting the theme, an elegant little brass oil burner containing your guest's birthstone for a Bollywood party, a caricature of the party host in a themed setting all with themed reply cards. Others may be simply elegant, some taking the form of a relevant item, for example, written on the bottom of a baby shoe, 'your presence is requested for the first birthday of baby...' it is a both sweet and charming invite.

The invitations should be sent out as soon as you know you are having a party, I know most guests look forward to parties, and they will look forward to yours. There is a 6 week in advance, tradition for invites to be sent out, however, I believe that the chances are lessened of your special guests being able to attend the party, the longer you leave the sending out of the invitation. Always make sure you put on the invite how to reply, also add special email or fax number and RSVP card.

One party giver really did want to make a great impression on his guests so a photographer was sent to every guest's office or home to get snap shots of them. The guests did not know the reason someone was taking their photo in this manner. These snap shots were then set into a customised wanted poster, and sent out to them as invitations, every guest turned up to that party, they knew from the start it was going to be something very special.

If it is a large function or you do not want to collate the 'can come' and 'can't comes', you can organise with your party planner to do this service, it can be a huge job, as the collation will also have to take into account special dietary needs, changes from yes to no and back again, liaisons with the caterers and often if guests are coming from abroad, advise on travel and hotels. It is a good idea to put maps and lists of hotels, nearest train stations and approximate travel timings, all in with the invitations. It will save a lot of time for your guests and be much appreciated. It is also especially nice if you organise special rates at local hotels and put cab firms on stand by.

Joint Parties

Celebrations and birthday parties tend to be the main reason for joint parties. There is always great fun in deciding the theme, as friends tend to take a long time to agree upon it, and probably have been planning the party a long time in advance. When the theme is decided, it is generally very focused and often unusual and inter active, as both parties have compromised on the event to suit both their imaginations. The benefit of joint parties is the budgetary savings on such things as décor, venue, and the entertainments, though if you have double the amount of guests, whichever way you turn it, the food and drink will be double! Joint parties also give the guests and host an opportunity of widening their circle of friends.

Good themes for joint parties include The Blues Brothers with great music and fabulous clubby decor. East meets West, great for fancy dress, and Around the World for international glamour.

Party Moments

Mark Owen - Singer and Songwriter

The best party was a millennium party that I threw at my house. I had all my mates and family there. Some of which I had not seen for years.

I covered the garden in candles, and the house had a ceiling of blue and silver balloons.

A dream party would have to be locked up with a bunch of friends in a place like Theme Traders, all the props and costumes would be great!

Lighting

Mood lighting can set the whole scene. Many people only use lighting to decorate the party.

White walls washed with changing moving lights will create the mood over the evening. Up-lighting to props and decorations brings them alive, gold coloured up-lighters pointing to a 7ft gold award statue makes it stunning. Green and blue spots amongst pools of greenery and palm trees enhance them further and add intensified focal points. Pink and amber directional lights' flooding a ceiling, always radiates a warm glow on people's skins. Beware though of using green or blue lights shadowing guests, as those colours tend to make skin look pasty not radiant.

Lighting can make or break an event, if the lights are to bright the atmosphere may be lost, to low and you cannot see the menu!

Always use a professional lighting company if the venue requires extra power and distribution, as it is both a serious and dangerous thing for amateurs to mess around with.

There are many lighting companies around, however very few are 'creative'. Unless you are getting the lighting through your party planner make sure you see the quality of work they have done before, check out their insurance and make sure they say everything has been pat tested for safety.

For small jobs if you are setting up the décor yourself you can hire some up-lighters, which simply need plugging in, add a coloured gel to the front to create the colour. The gel is a sheet of coloured film that sits in a holder away from the light. Always use power breakers on all plugs and remember to organise plenty of extension cables that will need taping down to the floor for safety.

Linen

It is very nice to bring the linen into the style, theme and design of the event.

It must be impeccable. Whether it is crisp and white or polka dots, the cloth is seen close up for a long time. Even if you like white linen a slip cloth or small element such as glass beads or a sprinkle of glitter in a contrasting colour takes away from whites starkness.

With linen anything goes, huge paw prints stencilled across a green table say a Jungle party, ribbons stretched from all sides in red white and blue say French, hessian says rustic. Different colour cloths around the room in primary colours with matching coloured chair covers and napkins say Circus and completely change the image of the room. Use flags as slip cloths, and organzas as overlays, be adventurous, many guests spend most of their time at the table and feel it is their base.

If you have organised the linen make sure that you have arranged for someone to put it on, most caterers will add a charge for putting on chair covers as it is extremely time consuming.

Chair covers are incorporated into linen, as they are part of the make up of the table. Black always looks smart and can be dressed to any theme, tattered red fabric salutes Hell, silver sashes for 1920s, white bows for black and white schemes. Always check the size of the chair before ordering the chair covers, as they may not fit. Napkins can be arranged in all shapes and decorated to complement the table. Tied with rope and with sea shells dangling from the ends, the napkins take on an Underwater theme; fanned out and set in a glass with a red rose portrays Phantom of the Opera.

Wedding linen tends to be more classic using soft tones and pinks or ivories; these are generally in keeping with the brides dress and colour scheme.

Look-a-likes

Elvis Presley, Julie Roberts, Sean Connery, Hugh Grant. Mick Jagger, Bill Clinton, Marilyn Monroe, The Blues Brothers, and Tony Blair, celebrities are certainly better than Look-a-likes. If you can get celebrities to come along in person - if they're alive - that's great. They usually tend to come for one of three reasons, because they are your friends, because they are supporting a charitable cause, or for the exposure they will receive. If they are not available in person or because of budgetary constraints, look-a-likes are an excellent second best.

Look-a-likes come in all shapes and sizes. Marilyn is always popular, singing happy birthday or jumping from and oversized cake, while the amazing Chinese Elvis can sing like the king and wears a padded fat suit. Decide carefully how and when to use them, whether for a reception meet and greet or for a special surprise, maybe a Charlie Chaplin antic performed during the courses.

One rather unexpected incident occurred when we were running the Christmas grotto at a shopping centre in Queensway. We were providing Santa Claus and all his elves. On the opening day of the grotto, a full structured press launch had been arranged, and lots of publicity created around the fact that Santa was going to fall from the sky. A keen climber who actually worked in security there, volunteered to abseil dressed as Santa, from the top level to create a fantastic photo opportunity for the press and to WOW the audience. The idea was that he would stop at each floor. Unfortunately every time he swung into the floor he somehow caught his long white flowing beard in the ropes and it got tangled, and so was unable to swing out again! This was solved by me rushing down to each floor as he swung in and having to cut off the bit of his beard caught up. By the time Santa reached the bottom there was nothing left except a tiny little unkempt bit of beard, the paparazzi were watching and taking photos as were hundreds of people, then one little boy set everyone laughing when he said very loudly "that's not Santa mummy, Santa has a beard!"

Party Moments

Dame Tanni Grey Thompson - Paralympic Gold Medallist

The best party I have ever been to was my wedding reception... the great thing about wearing a big white (or in my case gold) dress was that you get to pick the music all night and better than that I got to arrange it all (which I quite enjoy) so pretty much everything was the way I wanted it. I got to pick my favourite food, favourite friends, etc... no one can say no to you when you are the bride!

What made is so cool was that I got to do it all - I do like organising things.... I did make a schedule for the day which annoyed some of my family - so they knew where everyone had to be and when.

One of the best thing was that we put disposable cameras on the tables - it cost a bit to develop them but they were great photos of the wedding.

My dream party would be a nice bar-b-que somewhere warm, with my family, and me not having to do any of the cooking or the washing up.

Marquees

There are huge varieties now available, from witches hats to clear span to double deckers. The style you decide on should reflect both your budget and scheme. One of the best decorated marquees I ever saw was at a Venetian party, the marquee had been elevated and had a canal going through its centre, with live fish, gondolas, and elevated terraces with hanging grapes and vines, all set under a beautiful star cloth sky. Clearly this event was not a do it yourself job and was a high budget well designed professional affair.

It is always important to view the portfolio of marquee companies, as all too often the quality is not great, they can be old, musty and dirty and have creased linings; try to see one up, or at least see the quality. We worked in a marquee in Holland that had been put up by the client two days before we arrived; it was smothered in daddy long legs! Perhaps the theme should have been 'Bugs'.

The marquee companies will offer you further services such as flooring and carpeting, power, toilets, distribution, drapes and lighting, it is better to work out carefully which of these services you actually want from them or whether you are going to get them separately or from your party planner. They normally sub contract in anyway, and tend not to be experts in those fields.

Some companies have incredible state of the art marquees and take a lot of pride in their product, they arrive on time, will trouble shoot and are completely efficient and have a back up service.

Pay attention to detail; make sure you see specifications and images of all elements you require prior to confirming or you may end up with builder style loos, noisy heaters and uneven floors! The marquee size you choose will be related to the function you are holding and a carefully planned floor plan will make sure you have the right amount of space to accommodate everything comfortably. If you are having caterers and performers do not forget you will need adjoining marquees.

Music

This plays a very important part, and I can honestly say that I have never attended an event without music. String quartets are wonderful and subtle, jazz musicians are great fun and usually have a very varied repertoire, there is also the added bonus that they can easily move around with their instruments, you can even get jazz musicians on stilts for added visual impact. Background music themed to the event is great, Chinese classical musicians for Chinese New Year parties, pianists for Victorian, Didgeridoos for Australian. We recently arranged a 'Catch Me If You Can,' party where, all the music related to flight such as 'Fly me to the Moon', interjected with the sound of plane engines. It caused quite a stir. As guests entered the dining area the engines revved louder for take off, and the guests all got very excited.

Beware of using such special effects too much, try to use them for high impact only.

Musicians need to be well looked after and well briefed; they need exact details of what is expected from them. They can hold the key to really getting the party mood going.

Musicians are often incredibly versatile as was seen at one event where we needed a band to fit in with a Rocky Horror Theme. Well with no such thing available, we talked to a great cover band that we work with regularly and persuaded them that, not only would they really enjoy learning a whole new repertoire, but would also really enjoy dressing the part! They came over and had costume fittings, suspenders, tailcoats and hats, learnt the music, words, and rehearsed extensively.

Then came the night of the event. We had provided a make-up artist and innocently had not mentioned it to them! Six grown men stood there in suspenders and tops and refused to have make-up put on. It was only when one of the crew actually said they look ridiculous in their outfits without make up that they finally agreed...phew.

Nightcaps

Nightcaps were originally meant to help set you to sleep, though rumour has it that you then wake up in the middle of the night wide awake, I personally have no experience of this!

Wonderful for those long parties, one o-clock in the morning and there is nothing better than a nightcap accompanied by breakfast and yummy cakes. Special areas can be set up for nightcaps, chill out rooms are great. Consider changing the reception that was earlier serving wine and beer, into a traditional gentleman's club with drinks served by usherette girls who can roll cigars.

Unusually decorated and themed spaces, set in quieter surroundings, each specialising in a particular style of nightcap, are fun and work well, try for example hair of the dog, though 1am is a little early for them! Espressos laced with brandy, and specially created tequila tasters are always popular

I have always found that when events extend till the early morning, having some entertainers as we did for one client, coming in from midnight till four, can be great fun, and will add a new lease of life and frivolity to the party.

On one occasion we had a couple of Fawlty Towers style waiters, who were serving the nightcaps in a rather peculiar fashion. Totally in keeping with his role as an entertainer, one of the waiters pin pointed a rather arrogant guest, who actually thought the waiter was being difficult, this went on so long the guest got seriously irritated and went to see the host, to see why the waiter kept bringing him the wrong drinks, and then drinking them himself.

He let the host know the calibre of the staff he had employed, as he really thought he was inefficient and taking liberties! He did however see the funny side when everyone started laughing at him.

Organisation

Your party should be organised efficiently from an early stage, and the invites sent out. It is the only way to assure that your guests are free for the occasion. Most people lead hectic lives and many travel extensively; book them early as they may have commitments months in advance.

You will also need to book up the performers, caterers, marquee hire, and facilities well in advance. The chances of getting any of the services you really want, booked at the last minute are about zero in peak periods. Apply the same to your party planner, if you are using one, leave plenty of time for them to organise everything, as they all also need to organise their schedules and if they are good, they will have had bookings for months. Leaving everything to the last minute really works against you, unless you are totally flexible, in which case Lady Luck will provide you with a great event, though not necessarily to your exact specification.

If you need to buy, make or hire special decorations organise them as soon as you know you are going ahead with the event, trying to scramble around at the last minute is both irritating for you, stressful, and takes the enjoyment out of organising the party.

I worked on a great Circus event which was staged at a beautiful mansion, nearly every detail had been considered and it was truly a spectacular scene, one little detail had been overlooked, and that lead to an unfortunate incident, some young elephants had been brought in. The elephants came with a trainer and were put into a lovely front garden, designed like an orchard, so the guests would pass them as they entered the marquee, this was all fine until the elephants started getting hungry, up went their trunks and down came branches of beautifully manicured ornamental fruit trees. With the succulent fruit in mind, and the guests arriving at the same time, and the fact the elephants simply would not move, it was decided to leave them, and replace the trees after the event!

Outdoor Parties

In general it is always advisable to have the option of some sort of cover or awning as the weather can be so unpredictable, cover needed if too hot, and cover needed if wet. You also need to remember that facilities have to reflect the amount of guests you have. You will need external loos available unless you are happy about everyone traipsing through your house. Allow for separate catering tents and power facilities. If you are having a fairground and marquees, the contractors will need to set up on flat ground otherwise you may end up with extra costs to level the floor.

On that note I would advise anyone thinking of having a large-scale external event to make sure they use event planners that can prove they understand the scale of the commitment. It is not for the faint hearted and needs specialist knowledge, and an understanding of the great outdoors. Remember marquees can blow away in heavy winds, one we know went two miles!

A good example of keeping your fingers crossed, and hoping the weather is good, which is something we prefer not to do, was a large event we annually sponsored for 9000 guests. The event for Great Ormond Street Hospital, is a fundraiser, with the theme of Peter Pan. It is usually spread all over Kensington Park Gardens. It was decided that no marquees would be provided, as the cost implication would have been immense. I mention this as a new set of unusual considerations occur with an outdoor party of this style, such as the provision of special vans for the hundred performers to get made up and costumed in. Security, as all their belongings were also there was extensive extra and security was needed in each area, although we did actually have some guests taking the hanging fairies and feathers in Tinkerbell's field. The distance to the loos often meant going to the other side of the park, which meant extra performers to cover the themed areas. This event was a huge success for Great Ormond Street hospital and has resulted in it becoming a 'must go' children's party.

Party Planners

Choose very, very carefully.

There are many around all the time, but it is only worth going to a party planner that is substantial and has a reputation. Visit their offices, view their portfolios and bouquets from previous events, talk to them about small details initially, to ensure that they are experienced enough to interpret your brief and guide you. Many party planners fail every year, as they do not understand that they are ultimately taking responsibility for a very important occasion, and often every element of it, they should be troubleshooting non-stop for all sections of it and arranging every minute detail. Bearing in mind that a risk assessment for a venue can be twenty pages long, the time involved for every aspect is huge, they need extensive insurance coverage and lots of endurance, as they tend to work very anti social hours and exceptionally long days.

Their attention to detail will need to be perfect and they need to have excellent contacts and back up facilities in case of a problem.

On top of that they will need cash flow to prepare for the event, pay deposits to caterers, production companies, musicians, venue etc. This initial outlay cost can be immense and if they are unable to undertake this commitment then they will be unable to produce an event the calibre you require.

Good and well known party planners are worth their weight in gold, bad ones who have little or no experience or your friends who simply think it will be fun, or who say 'I have arranged a party at University' or 'with a committee' or organised a party for other friends, rarely have the knowledge to take on a large detailed event which in reality needs to be run like a military operation.

Performers

These come in all shapes and sizes. Little ones who squash up in boxes, hanging ones dressed as vampires who scare your guests, funny ones for a warm up after dinner, meet and greet who welcome your guests dressed as singing flower girls and wanton sailors, and speakers who will, if you choose them wrongly, bore your guests to tears. Whichever you choose make sure they understand that they are there to entertain your guests and not to party themselves, brief them on the special guests to make a fuss of. The timings are imperative, let them know if things are running off schedule. Whenever possible give them a contact to report to, make sure they know the layout of the venue and walk them through their performance area.

If they are meeting and greeting guests have them in position twenty minutes before the first guest is due to arrive and discuss how they are going to greet them.

All too often you find performers drinking, smoking and inter mingling at the event itself, unless you have expressly invited them to do so, make sure to brief them otherwise. Give them their own space to change and prepare in, make sure there is food and drinks for them. Celebrity acts will have a contract which will cover all their requirements right down to the last bottle of water required, read the contract carefully or you may have a rather upset performer on your hands.

At one event we were supplying a dunking bath game where you threw a ball at a target and if you hit it someone was dropped into a bath full of water. We decided, as this needed tough people, .wrestlers would seem to be the ideal choice, so we contracted the services of a group of well known mud wrestlers. They were quite uncontrollable and could not grasp that they were not guests at the party, I ended up having to verbally kick them out, with the help of two very scared guys. Always bear in mind that it is better not to have the activity or performer if they will not co-operate.

Photography

A great memento of an event. Unless the photographic rights of the event have been sold exclusively to a glossy magazine it is a shame not to have a pictorial record. Many photographers offer a service taking pictures in a themed area, set up to catch the guests as they arrive.

When taken early in the evening guests can get the photos as they leave, these often need to be paid for, and are usual at charity functions, otherwise they are usually available later at a specific web site set up for the event. They can be purchased and down loaded over the Internet.

There are speciality event photographers, it is best to use them, as normal photographers will not generally be used to a noisy moving crowd, like everything else in the party planning business, check out the credentials, see their work or book through your party planner.

The photographic area should reflect the theme or style of the party.

At a Big Bang party we organised for the London Stock Exchange we produced a fabulous themed photographic opportunity, consisting of a backdrop we painted of all the original founders in black tie, we set them against the original interior of the Exchange. We created it in such a way that the guests actually looked part of the picture. It was very successful, and the photos were a great souvenir. Anyone seeing the pictures could well believe that they were friends of the founders.

Sepia Photo Booths are an activity, and also produce tinted photographs. Guests are invited to dress up in accessories and have their photo taken in the old fashioned way, styled to complement the party. The photos are instant, mounted and a good talking point; groups and individuals can participate. Watching you friends dress up is fun and a great spectacle.

Party Moments

Neil Phelps - Head of Media Banking - Coutts Bank

My best party... there have been a few! Lots of wild crazy and probably naughty ones in my youth, some very normal, sensible and sometimes tedious ones in my middle years and some fantastically varied ones in my working life. Well I do operate in the Media world after all!

None of these however compared to the 'surprise' sprung on me by my darling wife to celebrate my 50th in 2005. She successfully convinced me that our Tuesday night stay in a Hotel in the quiet of Norfolk with our beautiful 10 month old son and a peaceful day relaxing together was the treat I was expecting. On the morning of my actual birthday (still in bed getting my presents!) I had a call from my 25 year old son who was travelling the world and I had not seen since he left 9 months earlier. He was in Australia and I was thrilled that he had made the effort to call me. Then my 20 year old daughter called followed by my 23 year old son. The family scene was complete!

My wife's big surprise present. Wow! A week's bone fishing in Mexico with one of my best fishing mates. Fantastic! The dream holiday I had talked about but in my heart thought I would never do. I was speechless and duly thanked the wife with all the energy I could muster!

After a lovely family meal, back to the house a few scotches and bed. Birthday over!

Not quite. My daughters' birthday was 4 days later on the Sunday and it was her 21st! On the Saturday I was told to spend quality time with my baby girl and take her shopping in Cambridge, buy lunch and make her feel special. I do my duty and when we return home… big rush cos we had been out too long and we were in danger of being late for the restaurant where we were to have a 'quiet' family meal to mark my daughters coming of age. I was told we had to do it early because when the boring but necessary family bit was over, she was off to the local nightclub to boogie away through to the small hours with her very much younger mates.

On arrival at the village hall car park… it was full of cars! I though 'something fishy going on here'. No time to think and hurried from the car demanding explanations, being fobbed of with drivel and almost physically forced first through the entrance door of the Hall.

Wow! Nothing less than a 100 people waiting for yours truly to make his entrance. Lights on… and the obligatory Cliff Richard 'Congratulations' belting out from the stage as a collection of friends, family, even from my first marriage including my dearly loved ex father in law. work colleagues and probably some opportunist gatecrashers all cheered and whooped for the startled looking 50 year old standing amazed in the middle of the room.

I was burbling incoherently amidst the noise when my mate yelled in my ear to 'shut up. Your sons sent a message from Australia. Listen'. The room went quiet. I listened and stared at the stage where the words of my eldest son who I hadn't seen for nine months boomed from the speakers. Bless him…he had made the effort and I stood staring, listening and wishing he was there.

From behind the curtain he stepped, microphone in hand. That was it. Couldn't hold back anymore and the 50 year old burst into tears as eldest son jumped from the stage, embraced me with a bear hug and was joined by son two, daughter, baby 'Callum' and the fantastic lady who had flown son one all the way from Australia to make my night complete. What a picture we looked. How could you top that? Fantastic.

My dream Party? Now this is difficult. What chance the wife reading this book? I have to err on the side of caution so my innermost thoughts will have to remain a well preserved secret save for those who already know!

It has to be open air with a climate to match and a scene to die for. Either the mountains, the wild or a sun kissed beach location with the clearest blue water and golden sand around.

It would have to be all day and all night, so lets kick off with a fabulous family breakfast at which I can indulge in the excitement of opening cards and presents and squealing with delight at every stage.

Morning activity before lunch should include some leisurely activities such as walking, swimming, scuba diving, power boat racing… just lots of great fun!.

Lunch. Lets pull in the rest of the family including all still breathing distant relatives and close friends. Gotta be a fantastic Barbecue affair with roasting pigs, lambs and chickens with oodles of champagne and wine. Let's have a variety of entertainment going on as well. Magicians, jugglers, acrobats oh and a rerun of the 1966 World cup final highlights (or 2006 if we win it!).

For mid afternoon, lets be wowed by Paul Carack and Mike & the Mechanics. A solo during their break by the gorgeous Dido should suffice to complete the pleasure of music mixed with wine in the company of friends and family.

Gotta be a proper party atmosphere so lets give it a theme. A beach party and 60's and 70' style! Time for draft beers and spirits. Need a disco and someone funny enough to carry it off. Resurrect Chris Tarrant!!

Running seafood, curry and Chinese buffet please!

Lots of dancing so need to import gorgeous scantily clad ladies to gyrate provocatively somewhere near me (sorry Mrs P!). Couple of guys as well I guess…

Now here's the challenge. Madonna as the star act preceded by Kylie with Queen reformed as the middle act. Heaven!

By my reckoning that should get us through to the early hours and I will be absolutely dead on my feet but with memories to recall for the rest of my days.

Now for the slightly naughtier version…

Place Settings

Depending on the type of food you are serving and the theme you are portraying the table setting should be planned accordingly. There is a great choice of cutlery plates, glasses and serving dishes available for hire. If you are paying separately for the settings it is a good idea to have a choice. This may not be more expensive than going with the style that is offered initially by the caterer or venue. If the settings are already included in the price there can be a substantial difference.

There are many ways to customise place settings, simply adding a red rose across a black plate says Romance; use gold cutlery to create a sumptuous style banquet; glass under plates with huge tropical leaves, and the guests name inscribed on them in gold leaf is a lovely personal touch; multi coloured glasses for each setting says summer; tin plates and white mugs are ideal for 1940s, square white plates for Modern chic; under plates in slate for Jurassic and in bamboo for Thai.

When you have decided where you want guests to be seated, always make sure that their name is spelt correctly in front of their place. At a Spanish event write it on an open fan, for an elegant affair get the name written in beautiful calligraphy on grained paper.

Some venues have existing lovely in-house place settings. The Dorchester Hotel is a good example of somewhere it may be better to add decor rather than completely re-invent the setting. Annually, there is a fabulous ball there called the UK and London Date Book Ball. The event is for those connected to events and charities, it is an incredibly well organised sumptuous affair. The theme has always been fun, such as Board Games one year, and Underground Stations the next. This sets the scene for every table to be individually designed by the table sponsor. The table settings are always spectacular, and so is the table decor, one table in particular sticks out in my mind: a track was laid in the table, Paddington Bear rotated, and a train circumnavigated in front of the guests.

Power

Pow all the lights have gone...

When you are lighting a venue, marquee or home, check out the power availability, discos, catering equipment and lighting can and will use a lot of power.

This is something to consider at an early stage as generators may need to be brought in, distribution boards and leads will need to be laid, all this requires a qualified electrician/lighting engineer. You or your party planner will need to tot up the amount of power required for each of the elements and then ensure enough is available, and lots to spare.

It is always valuable to have back up power and generators available, even at the extra expense.

I was at one event where the power stopped; the caterers suddenly had no power in their ovens, the reason was the power requirement for the disco lights far exceeded the amount that had been allocated to specification. The power had been assessed very carefully and there was no reason at all for a shortage, after a mad panic, followed seconds later by an investigation it was found that the disco people had decided to upgrade their lighting rig to a more powerful one, nice thought... or maybe not, this information should have been passed on prior to the event, now we had a problem, no food or no disco. With a careful juggling act the lights for the disco were left partially off till the food had been eaten and the ovens no longer in use, a lot of trouble for a little extra power.

All the power should be on circuit breakers, if one trips the lot can go, remember to have separate power breakers on each electrical plug, not just on the end of the extension lead, it will make it much easier to identify any problem.

Props

Props really enhance a party. I have never ever been to an event, which has not used some style of prop. The use of props should always be maximised, light them, set them at an angle, show them off, they are going to create the focal and talking points of the event.

Go for large props that are easier to handle, high impact, and that make a statement, rather than small-scale props that need a lot of creativity and generally need to be put into displays to really work. A Wurlitzer jukebox, a statue of Elvis and neon lights say Rock and Roll, and are easy to place. Ten skeletons dressed as pirates, a galleon backdrop and series of huge ships wheel say Pirates of the Caribbean. Life size polar bears, a 9ft igloo and flaming icebergs depict the icy world of the Great North. Oversized toadstools, flamingo croquet, and waiters dressed as playing cards describe Alice in Wonderland, add a walk through Alice book and you really are entering different a world.

You can go as far as you want into the styling and theming of the event. View the props and get images to save disappointment; make sure you know the sizes and weight of the items; ensure they will all fit through the doors and into lifts. Do this entire work prior to booking any props. Make sure you understand what you have booked. When I started Theme Traders with David my brother, we used to hire the decorations for the events we organised from TV and film companies. The props always needed to be re painted and touched up, as they were used in a different manner, and on film they did not need to be pristine, as they do, if they are seen close up. The low quality of them was one of the factors that made us start to make and commission our own props, which are now always kept in impeccable condition, and touched up before going out for any event.

The moral of the story is, as mentioned before, check out the props prior to hiring them.

Remember, set decorations are fabulous as talking points and will certainly set the scene.

Prepare Prepare Prepare.

If you are throwing your own party keep an up to date 'to do' list, prepare in advance and do not leave anything to chance. Get everything down in writing. When you are using suppliers, make sure contracts are in place, and payments and deposits have been made. Specify early timings for arrival for all contractors, so you will not panic. In the case of a large event, start set up days in advance.

If you are using a party planner ask for regular updates, do not ask them about every conversation they have had with suppliers. Listen to their advise, they have probably created hundreds and hundreds of events. We actually did 55 events and prop hires one day over Christmas last year!

Party planners are the professional party throwers. If you have chosen them well they should ensure that you will have a totally stress free event.

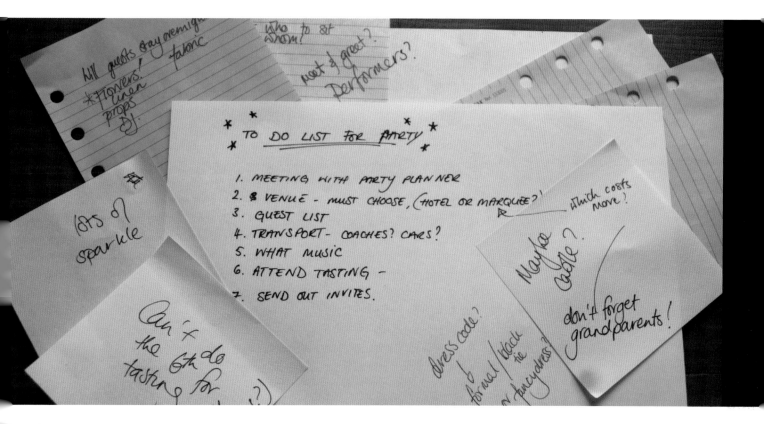

With an event of any size it is extremely important to be aware at all stages of the immense preparation required, always start at the beginning, how many guests, how much to spend, reason for the event. If you prepare the party knowing the answers to those questions the whole process will be easier and simpler to realise. The analytical preparation at this stage, will save you having to cut back and totally re think at a later stage.

We always take extra kit and props on jobs as something can always go wrong, and we also have crew at the premises on stand by. One job went absurdly wrong when a conference that was supposed to finish at 5pm for a gala at 7.30pm did not finish till 6.30pm! We ended up bringing down an extra eight crew from Theme Traders when we could not get in at the right time. It took an hour for them to arrive but as the back up plan was in place the extra crew made the event happen as normal. An hour of eight peoples time is equivalent to one person doing a days work, it can really make a difference.

Reception

Receptions at parties are pre dinner drinks, a warm up for a great event, a chance to chat with colleagues and old friends, to catch up on news. At celebrity and charity functions it is a great opportunity to people watch. Receptions also gather your guests together so they can sit down at the same time for the meal. Always consider some form of light entertainment at the reception.

Most people will have travelled a distance to visit you; make sure there are drinks constantly flowing and inviting canapés being served from beautifully decorated trays. Ensure champagne is always served cold; as with white wine, warm champagne is not nice, pour it out at the last minute, or have prepared part filled glasses and top up with fresh cold bottles. If you are serving canapés make them easy to eat, gooey drippy ones served with no serviettes are not fun and can be extremely embarrassing, skewered canapés with small dips are great

A reception can also mean a drinks party that tends to serve champagne, wine and orange juice. It is a good idea to have a focal point, perhaps a stunning stylish bar and characterised costumes for the catering staff, reflecting in some manner the reason for the reception.

Receptions can be held anywhere; they usually have a specific purpose such as the opening of a venue or hotel, the launch of a new building, or perhaps a special welcome for an important person or dignitary. Name badges are also valuable if there is a business reason for the event, otherwise you may never know who you are talking too, and miss a networking opportunity. Hosts to meet and greet, generally chat and give information to guests, are very valuable, as this style of event tend to be slightly more purposeful than an ordinary party.

Up to an hour is a good time for a reception, though in general allow 45 minutes, more often than not it will run to an hour by the time the guests have actually been seated.

Red Carpet Treatment

What a welcome, generally only for royalty but if it is there for me, I must be very special!

It is a wonderful hello and it really makes your guests feel important. Red carpet does not tend to cost a lot and can be used in a variety of lengths to suit your venue. Ropes and stanchions set alongside of it really add to the flavour, place two dressed flame lights at the entrance to the building and you have an amazing Wow factor. Finally, add a follow spot and you really are in Hollywood.

As an alternative to traditional red, vary the colour or use corporate colours and print the carpet with a logo or message. If your event is themed bring the entrance into the scheme, silver stanchions, black ropes and black carpet for a swishy cocktail party, rustic thick rope and wooden stanchions for a Victorian evening, silver stanchions, blue ropes and white carpet for nautical event.

I am delighted to say that the queen has walked down our red carpet on many occasions.

We recently sponsored a BA graduate at Central Saint Martins College of Art and Design. She used only our red carpet as her final degree show - so there you have it - Red Carpet is Art.

It was particularly interesting talking to one of the tutors at the college who said he had spent hours hoovering it as it had been laid in the corridor so everyone could use it. It really became a huge talking point and had developed its own persona, obviously an extremely unusual, but well thought out conceptual exhibit. Maybe we can sell it on Ebay one day...

On that note if you are having a carpet do not lay it until the last minute and always have a vacuum cleaner to hand, especially if it is white or black as every mark will show. If it has to be laid in advance always put a plastic dust sheet over it till the last minute, it should be pristine for your VIPs.

Room Transformation

Are these really the cellars at Skibo Castle? Now a stunning nightclub with low dark wooden tables, velvet stools, decadent displays of delicious fruit, cascading gently from wooden platters, and a gold and glass metre high candelabra, it is a truly decadent sumptuous room to hang out in.

Room transformations may apply anywhere, any design of space can be created. Alcoves can be sectioned off to create more intimate room transformations, and speciality areas can be formed to fit the theme. Consider Around The World, visit a variety of different and exciting destinations, separate the room by star cloth into smaller exciting continents, inter-linked by a walkway, each with their own entrance and style. Visit the Americas with a Western town, a bucking bronco, a shoot-out and a Texan Saloon bar; next is Asia with its full sized dragon snaking amongst its guests in China town, glowing with neon lights and colourful food carts serving delicious dim sum.

Total room transformations are created to lead your guests into an imaginary world, to give them a new experience and a wonderful time. Makeovers are a treat, an opportunity to fantasize. Theming and production companies form these transformations, similar to producing a theatre show, and they need time to do the design, any construction and preparation. The only difference is that it is all for your event only. Theming and production companies will often have an event management division, the difference between them and a party planner is that they can produce most elements of the set in house and then use their skilled rigging crew to set it in place on the day, Party planners tend to contract most elements externally and bring in crew to run the event on the day.

Full transformations are hard to do on your own; they require speciality rigging equipment and a lot of attention to health and safety. Depending on the size of the room it may require a lot of time to put everything up. It takes two people twenty minutes to erect a freestanding backdrop nicely.

Room Setting

If you decide to do the transformation yourself, you may be better off hiring backdrops and elements that are totally freestanding and that will arrive with the equipment and rigging needed to put them up easily. Visit the company you will be hiring from and ask to be shown the best method to assemble the chosen props, this can be incorporated into the initial visit and will be valuable as you can organise alternatives if items seem too complicated or time consuming for you to handle. Images on the web, often look smaller on line than in real life.

The room setting has to work for you, it needs to be practical and portray the atmosphere you require. The setting can be altered easily, yet still simply and partially. Aim to give the tables a real focal point, add clever use of mood lighting, coloured candles, music, low level seating, or bar seating; for banquets long trestles doubled up and U-shaped look amazing.

Room settings may be designed to any style for the event; add a wooden bar and chesterfields - you have a club room for cigars and a serious chat... a chill out room has low tables, sofas and bubble pyramids.. a games room, with table footballs and air hockey.. a cocktail room set with tall stools and a stunning chrome bar, glowing in the neon 'Cocktail' signs' warm reflection.

At one event the whole room setting changed dramatically when the tables started collapsing as guests started to sit down, it was awful. The catering staff in the hotel had not secured the table catches properly when they erected them, and if the table moved more than slightly it started to collapse, Fortunately we had not left the premises yet, we were able to provide crew to go under the tables, on their knees, securing the catches as guests were still coming in, whilst the hotel crew were re-laying the fallen crockery and glasses from the collapsed tables. The hotel catering staff had not been given any training regarding the erection of the tables. Look what happened, a near disaster.

Party Moments

Jasper Conran - Designer

I've been to so many great parties it's hard to distinguish. I love a party with lots of new faces but I also love an intimate gathering of old friends. Of course I love the parties I throw most of all. Some hosts can never relax but not me. Why throw a party if you can't join in the fun?

I enjoy my own parties because I'm surrounded by people I enjoy. Some friends I only see at parties. That doesn't mean I value them any less – they're simply party friends. I don't need much of a wow factor. It's all about the people. Of course I can appreciate an extravagant event but I think one can accomplish more by focusing on details rather than grand statements.

My dream party would be all down to the attendees. All of my friends and family would have to attend. It would start as a garden party during the day and then become a raging disco at night.

On second thought – maybe I'd invite my family to the garden party only.

RSVP

Check a week before your event that you have received all the RSVPs back, if not call your invited guests and find out if they are attending or not. Caterers will charge for last minute cancellations, as they need to prepare and order the food. Tables look awful with spare seats. One year I organised a huge banquet at Grosvenor House for a long-standing corporate client. It was for 700 employees of their company. They did not want a seating plan they wanted the guests to be able to sit wherever they liked. The amount of guests coming had been collated by one of the secretaries by internal email responses.

Heartbreakingly, only 400 turned up out of the 700 who responded positively. The tables were patchy, with some full, some half empty and some with just two guests sitting at a table for ten. The bill for the event was not reduced because of the no shows and the wastage of food astronomical.

Party Moments

LINFORD CHRISTIE - Athlete - Olympic Gold medallist

The best parties I have been to are at Hotel Du Vin, a small chain of hotels in the UK. They have fantastic parties when they open a new venue. The hotels are always in amazing old buildings with real character. They lay on great food, have great live music, which along with a good mix of people creates great atmosphere every time. The food rooms were amazing - one for fish, one for meat and one for cheese - with the an amazing spread in each.

My ideal party would be a huge garden party with all my close friends and family. Plenty of food and drink for everyone and some great live acts such as Usher & Kylie.

84

Seating plans

Essential if it is a formal event, essential if it is for networking purposes, and a good idea for family occasions where you want to group specific people together; weddings, bar mitzvahs and charity functions. Not important for family days BBQs, buffets, and relaxed occasions.

The seating plan should be very clear, and should be cross-referenced against the name and table number or name. If it is a large function, have a number of plans at a distance from each other and very prominent in the reception area so there is not a queue when it is time to sit down.

It is always nice to present the plans in style, perhaps in a frame on an easel, or decorate a board with gold drapes. Themed parties allow more creativity; bring the plans in line with the rest of the event, a graffiti wall for Graduation parties, an oversized luggage label for a cruise theme.

Make sure the type is large, clear and easy to read.

Deciding who is to sit next to who is a serious job. You have to think about two things, firstly the guests' feelings, and secondly whether they are going to fit in with the other people around the table. If you can get the right mix of guests on the table it will ensure a brilliant party.

Often you may be putting guests together for a particular reason, for example, to set them up with each other because, as Cupid, you know they will really hit it off. Well it doesn't always work like that and a great idea for those situations is to move every male guest two seats round with the coffee, this does not break up the company completely but allows the guests the opportunity of both getting away if they want, and to make new contacts. It is particularly fun at intimate dinner parties at home and very useful at networking events.

Staffing

This can be taken care of entirely by a party planner, and on a medium to large scale event it is wise to leave it to them. If you are having caterers they will look after their own staff.

An alternative is to bring in agency staff. There are speciality agencies for everything in the events world. Book the staff for slightly more time than you anticipate. the event will take. They often have other jobs to go to, and you may find you have no-one left to help finish the job. Bear in mind that you will also be charged overtime if they stay to help after their contracted hours.

You will have your work cut out for you if you take this route. All personnel need detailed management, which means you need to have a lot of time available throughout the day for troubleshooting, and you must be able to work to your time schedule or you will end up stressed-out and running late.

Party Moments

Ian Fraser - Unique Venues

The best party I have been to was My daughters wedding reception held at Dulwich college. My daughter, her husband and all the guests thought is was the best wedding reception they had been to and the weather was spectacularly good, lots of guests were even sitting outside on the lawns of the college after 11.00 p.m. The setting, the perfume from floristry, the weather and the guests really enjoying themselves made the day perfect.

As I am not into loud music any more, my ideal is a small dinner party with my wife and 8 - 12 of our closest friends at the two Michelin starred Midsummer House by **the river** Cam in Cambridge on a fine summers evening.

Stage Décor

Definitely an important focal point. The band and performers will use this as a backdrop to their acts as it tends to be set behind the dance floor. Try and bring the decor into the theme and style of the event. A safe bet and nice background for any event is a star cloth. This is a flame retardant theatrical cloth inserted with tiny magical lights creating a starlight effect; often discos and bands will provide them as part of the service.

A simple and effective stylish stage can consist of a backdrop flanked by large-scale props on either side reflecting the décor of the room.

If you are on a low budget the stage should be one of the most important areas to pay attention to. Always make sure you light the stage décor with character and ambience matching the scheme.

A Grease backdrop flanked by silhouettes of Sandy and John Travolta; a Mexican Cantina backdrop with huge cacti set the scene for a Mariachi band. A river boat is a great background for a New Orleans style jazz band; a massive Union Jack for a Military band, with British Bulldogs on a stack of ammo boxes. Comedy and Tragedy masks lit in gold look stunning for any style of event and can be added to make a great stage.

One stage we decorated consisted of an amazing exploding balloon wall, which unfortunately partially toppled over when detonated! Someone had removed the weights from the back braces on the frame. We found out it was the venue's health and safety officer, who said afterwards that the weights had been in the way of anyone crossing backstage! This event involved a famous racing driver who, at that time had his leg in plaster; he very nearly ended up with another one in plaster. Everyone in the room thought it was part of an act, as he was on stage at the time!

Stage Sets

A stage set can be built for any event, like that of a theatre; it can be all singing and dancing or simply static. We once created an unusual rotating set for a launch party of a well-known washing machine manufacturer. It was set on a turntable, and at a given time, revolved to reveal a celebrity comedian in a question and answer situation, it was all very funny and got a lot of press. The response was a very rewarding experience, as it is not that easy to make a washing machine terribly exciting!

Lots of stage sets are used for different purposes throughout an event, for example an overhead or back-projected screen, may be used at an awards ceremony to show clips from various winners, later to show music or film video clips to accompany a disco. Lecterns are often used and come in all different shapes and sizes; you can cover them to match the style of event, and brand them in any manner you like.

Stage sets are primary focal points for any event and add greatly to the visual impact of the room. The set-up of the stage needs to be thought through carefully, in line with the overall concept and design of the event. Lovely stage sets can be simply designed and not over-complicated, even the smallest set that you could use at home will look stunning if you make it fit in with the styling.

Often at weddings and Barmitzvahs a family will have their table elevated onto the stage. It will normally be set against a well defined background; classical, beautifully dressed trellis and roses with arches at weddings. At Indian weddings the stage set is more likely to have ornate columns, huge dressed elephants, and decorative thrones. An Arabic style event may have a soft canopy above and drapes framing the whole table. Barmitzvahs are fun when the theme of the child is depicted in the stage set, James Bond, Sci-fi or the Bible, they all make a great scene for the special occasion.

Styling

Not all party hosts want 'theming', they can be often put off by the word. It may conjure up images of tacky props and decor, this thought is a fallacy, theming, designing, styling, setting the ambience are all really the same, though some include the implementation of the various elements of the party. The key is to fashion the party in a way that matches the image you want to project. The style of your party needs to be achievable. Review the space, design, practicality and cost implications. Set a special budget for the styling, not just what is left after everything else has been motioned.

There has been a trend of boutique hotels popping up all over the world, these have been 'themed' in a modern and often minimalist fashion; though currently the style is veering towards slightly more 'eclectic' and colourful schemes. These are in effect designer hotels that have been themed to fit the trends. Parties also follow, they go in cycles, following fashion and current affairs.

Stylish parties can be achieved by simply colour co-ordinating furniture and matching floristry.

Delightfully styled parties, where you want the theme to be linked to a movie such as Star Wars, need to be designed and styled to portray the atmosphere, and echo the story; a Tatooine-style bar, futuristic space effects, Yoda and other wonderful performers complete the set, whilst a Harry Potter school feast takes place in a oak clad hall set alight by hundreds of flickering candles, roving ghosts and attended by Dumbledore.

Candles and Candelabras are very atmospheric at parties, and are ideal for styling. They come in all shapes and sizes, church candles amongst holly for Christmas, small tea lights in glasses for the base of table centres. Gothic-dressed candelabra for Weddings, candlelit Tiffany lamps for Burlesque.

Table Centres

Everything goes. Customised and logoed table centres are usually the choice for corporate events. Themed parties gain momentum by having a table centre in harmony with the overall style. Miniature goldfish in tall vases on mirrored bases replicate an Aquarium venue; a revolving mirror ball for the Seventies; huge feather displays with Venetian masks for Masquerade Balls; clapperboards and film cans for Award ceremonies; African spears for Out of Africa, stacked glitter dice for Monte Carlo. Flowers incorporated into the table centre can look wonderful. On some table centres, balloons suspended from the centre piece add colour and overall visual impact to the room.

If you wish to elevate table centres, use low plinths or tall stands. Make sure that the width and height of the table centre will not obstruct the view guests have across the table. It can be very disappointing to end up with a table centre that is visually obstructive, so see a sample first.

Perspex stands are perfect for elevating any table centre as you can see straight through them, and they are also very stylish. Candles are always atmospheric on the tables. Check you are allowed to use them if you are holding your party in a hired venue, as a lot will no longer let you use live flames. You can get battery candles and beautiful LED lights set in candles as an alternative.

Table centres that contain presents, gifts and novelties are entertaining. An upturned sparkling glitter top hat, filled with tinsel wigs, party poppers and blowers are eye catching and will get your guests excited at the thought of dressing up. Though it may take a few drinks, they will probably all participate at some stage! Confetti bombs can be exploded in the middle of the table, leaving a scattering of shimmer foil. Table centres can be edible, goldfish bowls full of candy bracelets for Barbie parties; sand buckets full of candy canes and rock for Seaside events; oversized lollipops stuck into a colourful glass relate to Charlie and the Chocolate Factory; bubble gum machines full of peanuts are ideal for American Independence Day and Sports Bars.

Theming

Choose the theme, and take inspiration from everywhere. If you cannot come up with good ideas for your theme try word association - write down twenty related words and use them in the design. Think about what the event is for, and how you want it styled. Is it for fun, a launch, a birthday, a Christmas party, an award ceremony or wedding?

Each reason provides you with another set of themes available. Eras are great for theming, a 30th anniversary brings you to the Seventies and Austin Powers in his hey day, with mini cars, giant lava lamps, and velvet suits; the room is set with funky seating and a flashing dance floor, all completely transformed in bright colours with a huge rotating circular bed covered with shaggy fur fabric, consider adding mind bending circles, good company, a DJ with real decks and you are living it. Shagadelic style.

Theming and Styling add a wonderful magical element to all events. At a large scale party, the theming can add up to immense sums, and it needs to be perfect; use professionals where possible.

Celebrating a company's 100th anniversary takes you to Cockney England; take a stroll through the cobbled alleys and visit colourful street markets; Covent Garden for delicious desserts; Smithfield's where you taste the best cut of meat. Add a custom backdrop depicting the fruition of the company, and you will bring about a sense of realisation and interest for the guests.

A little bit of theming does go a long, long way. At a small intimate dinner party, theming really adds to the tempo; theme the table for a murder mystery with a black cloth and large gold question marks; at a traditional Sunday lunch add a sparkle by hiring a fibreglass lamb for the middle of the table, include a green table cloth and with these small gestures, you have given the party a themed atmosphere, which will make it all the more memorable and fun for everyone attending.

Party Moments

Louis Mariette - Bespoke hat couturier

My favourite party was based on my philosophy...if you going to do it, do it properly in "full" decadent style!

The whole event was an explosion of signature purple! The road around the building was covered in purple carpet,scattered with rose petals, barrage of papparazzi, a "who's who" gueslist from Elton John to Zara Phillips... all of us stepping onto the alternative red carpet(Purple)! Bouncing and sashaying and stealing the limelight were the most over "fluffed up candyfloss" poodles that I had ever seen... even Eltons eyes lit up as he struck a pose with David (who was, I imagine was already thinking how he could see the fluff balls wearing a diamond encrusted Asprey collar back at their palace)!

Then again was it that wow factor or the fact that as you entered the "A" list shuffle to get in, up ladders were the most jaw dropping window cleaners topless in purple dungerees! Or the exotic purple cocktails or the sheer incredible store and products. Whatever it was, such great effort was made and I take my "hat" off to them!

My dream party would be the launch of my new perfume! Not too give too much away, however it would probably entail flying out the press and VIP guests to the most amaaazing outcrop limestone cliffs I found in Thailand, boating them through the exotic balmy night air and a light illumination never seen before. Hundreds of meters of fabric and petals would waft from the cliff tops as oversized flags waved around saturated with the scent, then... enough, enough information... I can't reveal the other exciting thoughts, you will all have to be patient and see if you recieve an invitation!

Transportation

When booking a venue or organising a home party take care to consider how your guests are going to get to you. Many will want a drink and though they may be able to drive there, they most certainly should not drive back. If you are a way out of a city, do a little research into local hotels and taxi firms, check availability and add a separate info note with names and addresses into the invitation, also add a small map, this will be gratefully received and give guests the opportunity of not having to worry about the distances involved.

If a lot of guests are coming from the same place you can even go so far as to book a train carriage exclusively for them, as was the case when I attended a party at Jasper Conran's beautiful country house. He had also arranged coaches to come at certain times to collect his guests to ferry them too and from the train station, very thoughtful and well received by all.

Overseas parties need further deliberation regarding the transport element. An invitation to a birthday lunch in Spain may not warrant the transport and accommodation expense to some guests. If you really want guests to attend overseas you need to give them a fuller invite, maybe take into consideration accommodation and breakfast, or organise the flight for them, When you make the event a 'must go' affair and it has a good reputation, it will be heaving, regardless of where it is held. Without these factors you may find there is a fall out, simply because of the costs involved.

Transportation at parties can be great fun, a boat down the river to the venue; a miniature train ride from the entrance to the picnic; a rickshaw ride for the bride and groom to their wedding reception a double decker bus collecting guests from their homes. Limos, with fully laden bars.

At one party we organised, forty guests were flown to Skibo Castle for a weekend party by private jet, a rather luxurious way to go, we drove up in our vans with the props, it took 16 hours...

Uniforms.

Co-ordinate the uniforms to the theme, the staff then become live props and this adds to the event ambience. Drape jackets for the 1950s; national costumes for any country around the world; Clogs and striped skirts for Holland; Sarees for Pakistan; lederhosen and long socks for Germany.

Simple high-neck Nehru jackets come in assorted fabrics, velvet for banquets, black linen for general use, they are a stylish change from the traditional bow tie and jacket. Include a turban along with a sash and it will take you to the Days of the Raj; a coolie hat goes to China. Blazers and boaters are perfect for jazz evenings, fairground events, Henley and summer brunches.

All parties can be spiced up with lovely staff uniforms. White satin tail coats and bow ties look amazing for Winter Wonderland and glow in UV lighting.

Uniforms are all costumes, yet the word costume sounds subtly more glamorous.
Full or part uniforms can be hired, black shirts, trilbies and white ties are easy accessories at a Gangster themed party, bouncers can even be costumed as American Policemen. Striped waistcoats and boaters put on over existing white shirts and black trousers are the best uniforms for a Summer Extravaganza.

We were commissioned to design and make a set of stunning, totally unique pale blue livery outfits for the waiters at Elton John's White Tie and Tiara Ball, a fabulous annual event in support of his superb Aids charity - The Elton John AIDS Foundation. The staff all looked wonderful, complemented by their powdered wigs. The reason we were asked to make the uniforms from scratch, was because over a hundred identical ones were required, and as waiting staff work so hard they need light, practical and impeccable clothing at high profile parties. Bear this in mind when organising staff clothing and do not give them heavy theatrical ones as they will end up tired and sweaty!

Venues

Venues may be anywhere and any space; fabulous luxurious hotels, traditional barns, historic houses or perhaps, simply a marquee in your garden. The choice is endless, and should be determined by both your budget and reason for the special occasion. A summer party is lovely in a marquee, a charitable high-profile fundraiser is best arranged in an elegant and well known venue where the quality can be guaranteed, and expectations can be exceeded with only a little effort. Birthdays for young people tend to be noisy, and the venue needs to be sound-proofed in some way or simply a bit out of the way to save problems with the neighbourhood. The party will probably go on till 3am, and still be providing drinks for those late night revellers who will soon need breakfast!

There is a wonderful range of venues now available. Nearly all venues have facilities either in-house or with external contractors to make the event a great success. So be adventurous...

Visiting the internet sites of venues can save a lot of time when deciding where to hold your event; floor plans, images of the venue and the variation in the types of events they have held, tend to be on-line. This can really help at the initial stages and save you a lot of time from having to visit the possible venues in person. Rates seem to be set, though most venues do tend to have flexibility and often go out of their way to secure the booking. It is well worth having a good chat with the banqueting manager at the first meeting and discuss what you actually need from them, so further down the line there are no hiccups. If you are having theming, bands, performers, lighting, and the venue is being used till an hour prior to the event, it may be worth finding a more compatible venue. The short set-up time will put immense pressure on everyone.

Setting up a venue for an event is in fact a military operation, attempted by many, and achieved by few. Put in writing to the venue any special requirements and get them to confirm back in writing They will advise you about all possibilities, or, you may find yourself having a rather tricky ride.

VIPs

VIPs can really make a big difference to an event, their attendance makes it more exciting for the other guests, and delights the press. When it is a fund raiser it is very, very valuable to the charity as their presence will definitely sell more tickets, and raise more revenue for the charities cause. If it is a celebrity private party, the guests will probably include many VIP guests anyway. The emphasis needs to be on security at all times, remember the gatecrasher at Prince Williams's party!

Many events require a special VIP area and someone to look after them for the duration of the event. If you have invited a VIP make sure you treat them very well, special attention is of the utmost importance. Always delegate the job of looking after these special guests to someone with charm and great organisational skills. At a charity fund raiser my father-in-law held in Belgium, Bill Clinton certainly had some special needs, somewhere to park his Boeing...

The value of a VIP at an event should never be under-estimated; it brings great PR and support.

In the music world there is always a VIP area for bands having an album launch for the press and industry. We decorated one VIP room with massive black-out cloths, huge crosses, and an electric chair, all at the request of the record company. This was for a rather famous band! They had extra security at the entrance to this area, even though it was a private room; everyone looked extremely chilled when they came out! They had many special guests in there all night, what a VIP room. We know the party was a success, as we had to do it again at their next record launch!

At another launch party we themed games, and provided fairground stalls for a band that had just had their first Number One hit record. We were asked if our performers would give away joints which had been had prepared in advance, as prizes on the activities; we politely informed them that we could be arrested for this, we suggested they found another means of distributing their prizes!

Wow factor

Make every detail at your party a Wow factor – bearing in mind that the first impression is the one that counts. Choose your theme and then make it come alive.

Start at the entrance. In a Castle have meet and greet knights on horseback; transform the front of your house into an African village; leave open an endangered species cage with a crazy escaped gorilla; consider the impact of a voodoo witch doctor dancing on a coffin, James Bond style.

Have a series of rickshaws waiting to take guests from the car park to the venue; light up a woodland path and see pixies and fairies sitting on toadstools with fairy chimes jingling all along the route; have children in rags singing renditions from Oliver Twist; or New York street musicians playing oil drums, while an American street vendor hands out miniature hot dogs at the entrance.

No rules here - 'horses for courses'. Let your imagination become reality, the attention to detail and creative ideas, will give you and your visitors something to remember for a very long time.

There is no wrong or right time to create the Wow factor, design the party with your guests in mind. Use the ideas most appropriate to the party. Pavarotti with dessert can Wow guests as much as Madonna will to the right audience.

The design of the tables, the shape of the glasses, unusual performers, speciality acts, stunning décor, amazing props, dancing water, indoor fireworks, laser shows, heliospheres, balloon rides, simulators, anything and everything can transform the party into something more than a normal affair, especially if it is presented with style and panache.

Create a visually magnificent experience for your guests and you have created the Wow factor.

What To Wear

As the host or hostess you have to give a lot of consideration to your clothing. When it is a themed event you may want a stunning outfit that really sets the scene for the event, make sure it is very special as your guests will comment immediately as you welcome them in. If it is not fancy dress, but black tie, try to add a little extra something to your outfit. For the girls; a flower in your hair to co-ordinate with the overall theme, for the men; an especially unusual bow tie. It is your party and you are the centre of attention when guests arrive – make yourself look fabulous and you will feel fabulous.

Guests should consider carefully the style of event and dress accordingly. I was invited once to a 'White Night' party and believed it to be an invite to dress in white; I put on badminton gear, a short skimpy skirt and vest, when I arrived everyone was in white tie evening dress, a little faux pas!

Party Moments

Michel Einhorn - Diamond Expert and Director of www.cooldiamonds.com

The best party I've ever been to was a Vampire party, held in my garden.

It was superbly spooky - my garden was transformed into a bit of Transylvania with scary realistic statues and a background tape of people moaning and crying. Amazing how much fun this was, somehow the sound of torture made our guests enjoy themselves!

The WOW factor was a vampire (an acrobat disguised) that hung upside down in a tree in front of our house and would jump on guests as they arrived. Terrifying for them, great fun for us!

I would love to have a party as the sun sets in the Namibian desert with just a few close friends..

Themes

Themes

This chapter is meant as a guideline and has initial ideas, to start the ball rolling for many possibilities within a party.

All the names of the themes can be changed to create a buzzy and memorable name, for your party. For example, India can be called 'Days of the Raj', Horror can be called 'Halloween' or 'Hammer House'. I have put the names in the simplest forms for ease and identification. Consider joining themes to create fun, change and excitement, try 'East meets West' or 'Hoe down at the OK Corral'.

Make the name of your party exciting, instead of 'Jungle' what about 'Rumble in the Jungle' instead of 'Military' try 'Forties Swing'. Remember anything goes. We did a themed party for Saatchi and Saatchi who named their event, which was actually a summer tropical style party, 'Life's a Beach' and everyone was given badges with that logo. It made the whole event more interesting and guests found the play on words very amusing.

All the schemes can be achieved in your house depending on scale, and can also be actually achieved anywhere, however some venues lend themselves to specific schemes and their existing decorations provide partial enhancement to the theme.

If your budget will allow you to create full transformation any scheme would lend itself to a blank canvas, an empty space, a warehouse, or a marquee. If budget is restricted simply add a few special props alongside styling and decor to make your event unique and memorable.

The storyboards are to set the scene for the idea, the synopsis is to clarify a few of the ideas, the party spec is a soft guideline to help with the initial step and possibilities for the structure of party. It does take into account that most parties will finish with discos. The music suggestions are for the initial meet and greet, the general background music and any speciality music overall to complement the whole party.

All of it is totally flexible and as everything else in design, subjective.

Addams family

Dare you pass through the tall iron gates and enter the Addams family home?... When the swirling mists clear you can see the tombstones and coffins in the garden, but are they occupied?... Inside everything is covered in cobwebs, and bats and spiders lurk in dark corners not lit by the black flickering candelabras... Find a boiling cauldron in the kitchen and an electric chair in the front room... See the family themselves immortalised in a creepy portrait... Just watch out for the scampering hand!

Ideal theme for Halloween; set a graveyard entrance, use dry
ice for effect, have coffins as occasional tables

Invites: Open coffin

Styling: Spooky, lots of green lights, tombstones, and cobwebs

Music: Eerie, old Hammer House effects

Drinks: Blood Transfusion

Performance: Characters from the family

African

Experience the desert plains and the steamy jungles of the mysterious African continent...
Take a safari expedition and see stunning wildlife: zebras, elephants, even a rhino;
just be ready in case he charges!... Head into the lush green jungle full of exotic
flora and fauna, but watch out for snakes amongst the hanging vines... See beautiful
African masks and statues and handle tribal shields and spears for yourself...
Have a go on the drums and check out the lions arriving in the deep of the night.

Put a rhino in the middle of your drive to make guests go around it. Use jeeps to shuttle guests. Use African traditional drummers, but be aware as they bring on the rain.

Invites: Mini African drum

Styling: Jungle, vines and animals

Drinks: Coconut cocktails, rum

Music: African Drumming

Performance: African dancers and African witchdoctors

Arabian Nights

Enter a world full of Eastern promise... Sample the delights of this exotic culture... Follow signs to the bazaar where the air is heavy with the scent of spices... See the beautiful brass ware, silks and materials for sale or even make a bid for a camel... Rest awhile and enjoy a hubbly bubbly pipe with friends... Eat honey coated sweets at low tables... Finally head out into the desert to see the stunning sunset over rolling sand dunes...

Create a Bedouin tent, give your guests fezzes and do not forget the full-size camel. Serve cous cous and mezzes from tagines on low-level tables and large cushions.

Invites: Palm leaf or a fez

Styling: Bedouin tent style with bazaar entrance

Drinks: Lychee Martini and Mohitos

Music: Arabic band

Performance: Belly dancers and snake charmers, soothsayers,
Ali baba meet and greet

Alice in Wonderland

Join all the characters from the classic children's tale for lots of fun and adventures...
Take a seat at the Madhatters Tea Party but be careful what you eat... See the caterpillar
sat on a giant toadstool and share his hookah pipe... Enter a magical world where
suddenly you become as tiny as Alice and all around you are giant objects... Play a game
yourself on the enormous chess board and meet the Queen of Hearts face to face...

A great theme for fun, very magical; the use of performers here a must, make all
your sets of tables and chairs different sizes, use a black and white dance floor.

Invites: Drink "with" me bottle

Styling: Very colourful and oversized, chess pieces, colourful topiary

Drinks: Pink Margaritas served from a tea pot

Music: Alice soundtrack, alternatively Alice in Ibiza!

Performance: Drag queen Queen of Hearts and Mad Hatter MC
Caterpillar with pipe!

Around the World

Follow in the footsteps of Phileas Fogg and take a wonderful journey around the world...Visit all the places you have ever dreamed of on the trip of a lifetime and enjoy the sights and sounds of a myriad of different cultures... Begin close to home with a taste of Europe... See famous landmarks like the Leaning Tower of Pisa or the Eiffel Tower... Travel to exotic locations such as China and India or experience the wonders of the heart of Africa... Relax on a sun drenched Caribbean beach or join the hustle and bustle of the streets of New York... The world is your oyster...

Try using a scheme like this for a buffet, theme each area to a different culture. It is great for large groups of guests and is an excellent icebreaker. Use hot air balloons on the occasional tables. Use any elements at all from any countries you choose.

Invites: Passport

Styling: Landmarks and ephemera from Around the World

Drinks: Anything goes, Saki, Beers, Tequila, Chianti

Music: Traditional, a Sitar player from India, Didgeridoo from Australia

Performance: Speciality acts from each country; French mime artists. Chinese dragon

Ascot

*Enjoy a day at the races at one of the most famous events in the racing calendar...
Pass through the turnstiles and enter the exciting atmosphere of the racetrack... On
ladies day join everyone in their finest clothes and see who has the most outrageous
hat... See the horses and their jockeys as they get ready to go... Maybe take a chance
and place a bet at the bookies' stands... Join the crowds at the starting post to see the
action or be there at the finish line... Then head to the bar to celebrate your win!*

Horse racing schemes fit beautifully into the season, dress the room in horse
racing backdrops, use a series of starting posts at the entrance, make sure that
your guests can have a punt on the horse racing on the screen centre stage.

Invites: Printed betting slip

Styling: Racecourse and horses, Champagne and strawberry stalls

Drinks: Steeplejack cocktails and Champagnes

Music: Jazz band

Performance: Race evening, jockey girls and tote makers

Atlantis

Under the sea find the watery home of the lost city of Atlantis... Here pillars lie broken, plinths and statues overturned... Beautiful shell cornucopias can be found on the sea bed alongside the anchors of lost ships... Look hard enough and you will find hidden treasure spilling from sunken chests... Lobsters, crabs and fishes make their home amongst the ruins... Balloons in silver, blue or transparent are everywhere like bubbles rising from the water...

Props from the classical range lend themselves to this scheme, it can be truly elegant, colour-coordinate the whole theme to white, silver and blue, use iridescent table cloths and white chair covers, scatter the table with shells. Water-effect projections look amazing on a white dance floor.

Invites : Map of Atlantis

Styling: Classical columns, nautical props, balloons and bubble columns

Drinks: Blue Lagoon cocktails

Music: Dolphin effects, string quartet – Handel's water music

Performance: Wandering and static mermen/mermaids

Australian

G'day mate! Throw some snags on the barbie, grab a cold stubby and enjoy some antipodean delights... Fancy yourself as Crocodile Dundee? Recreate the movie with yourself as the star, put on your corked hat and head to the outback to do battle with a mighty croc... Maybe you would prefer to sit back in the sun and watch some cricket or head for the sand and sea and enjoy a cool beer at the beachside bar...

A cool theme for a BBQ. Create a swamp area with crocodiles; use rustic wooden chairs and a bar from corrugated iron and driftwood. Set the tables with didgeridoo centre pieces and have aborigines tempting guests to play.

Invites: Corked hat that must be worn to gain entry

Styling: Swampy with crocs, heading down to cool beach area, Aboriginal paintings

Drinks: Prairie Oyster, Waltzing Matilda

Music: Didgeridoo, classic Aussie sing-alongs

Performance: Crocodile Dundee look a-alike, Aborigine body painters

Back to School

As the bell sounds through the halls, take a trip down memory lane as you go back to your school days... Put on the old school tie or play at b eing teacher in your gown and mortarboard... Keep out of trouble or you may be doing lines on the blackboard at the front of the class... Have fun in the science lab or in the school gym... At break time visit the tuck shop where the sweetie jars are always full... If you feel brave try out the school dinners in the canteen...

Encourage your guests to dress up, have a graffiti board for messages, make sure there is a schoolmistress with a cane to stop the guests from misbehaving. Use paper tablecloths and chalk to write with.

Invites: School Report

Styling: Panelled walls, classroom, blackboard, tuck shop, graffiti areas

Music: School Disco

Drinks: Blue Nun, mixers, spritzers

Performance: Headmistress and PE teacher

Baywatch

Enjoy your very own Californian dream... Lay back in your deck chair and watch the surfers ride the waves... Feeling lazy? Then just let others exert themselves playing volleyball on the sand... Head to the beach bar for a cool cocktail under the shade of a parasol and check out all people having fun, you may even spot Pamela herself!... Stroll along the beach at sunset and find beautiful shells, but watch out for any crabs that may be hiding!

Beautiful surfer types for meet and greet, consider a surf machine, and surf boards large shells will work well for canapés. Have massive sharks and dolphins then recreate a huge rip curl wave, and use as part of the bar.

Invites: Mini surfboard

Styling: Malibu beach side, surf boards, colourful parasols, lifeguard hut

Music: American pop, Venice Beach beats

Drinks: Malibu Bay Breeze

Performance: Surfers, oiled body builders, rollerbladers, Pamela look-a-likes

Blues Brothers

"It's 106 miles to Chicago. We've got a full tank of gas, half a pack of cigarettes, it's dark and we're wearing sunglasses. Hit it!"

Put on your hat and shades and recreate the famous Blues Brothers mission for yourself... Take a journey through the history of blues and soul with the boys... Black and white are the colours, with glittery guitars and musical notes all around and plenty of pictures of the stars themselves, Jake and Elwood...

Enter through a jail, meet the cops who present you with your Gangster hats, have a Blues Brother cover band and go for black and white.

Invites: Album Cover or Blues Brothers Shades

Styling: Black and white gangster and clubby atmosphere

Music: Blues and pianist

Drinks: Bottled beers, whiskey shots

Performance: Blues Brothers cover band, slinky hostesses

Brazilian Carnival

It's Fiesta time and temperatures rise as everybody gets hot! Hot! Hot!

Follow signs to Rio and let the Latin rhythms move your body and free your mind... Everywhere see shimmering glitter and bright colours... Beautiful carnival masks and tropical fruit heads are on display for all to see... Catch yourself some carnival beads... Cool off for a while with an exotic cocktail then get ready to party through the night as the carnival sounds fill the air...

Use Salsa dancers, have a huge costume parade, tropical displays all around, large masks and candelabra emphasizing the heat of the moment.

Invites: Coloured silhouette of a Carnival dancer

Styling: Purples, reds and golds, clashing colours and feather displays

Music: Salsa and Samba

Drinks: Pina Coladas and Baccardi classic cocktails

Performance: Salsa dancers, fire-eaters

Brighton Pier

Take a gentle stroll down Brighton Pier and enjoy all the seaside fun... Feeling lazy? Then take a seat in one of the colourful deck chairs and relax in the warm sunshine... Watch the activity on the beach where children play in the sand and sea... Have fun on the end of pier amusements... Try your luck at the modern games or enjoy the old fashioned penny arcade... Have your photo taken with your head through a peep-through board... If the sea air gives you an appetite visit one of the many food stalls for a tasty burger or some delicious candyfloss...

Create an old fashioned amusement arcade, use red and white extensively, have table centres made from buckets and spades and filled with customised rock.

Invites: Stick of Rock, inscribed with name

Styling: Red and white. seaside, old fashioned stalls and amusements

Music: Fairground, Honky-Tonk

Drinks: Slush Margaritas, ice cream floats with Martini

Performance: Music hall, strong man

Bollywood

Visit a distant land of exotic sights, sounds and aromas... And be transported onto the set of the latest Bollywood extravaganza... Rich colours are everywhere, Fuschia pink and burnt orange, in beautiful hangings, rugs and saris... Bejewelled elephants stand majestically... Escape the heat under parasols as pukha fans gently cool you...

Enter through sets of magnificent tusks, beautiful large carpet backdrops set behind Indian street stalls with appetizing samosa and bhajis for the reception, the Taj Mahal on the stage. Large elephants elevated on all sides of the dance floor. Indian dancing dolls for table centres, colourful sari-clad chairs.

Invites: Box with Indian sweets with invite engraved on lid

Styling: Exotic displays, eclectic colourful seating, brass ware

Music: Indian traditional

Drinks: Wine and Indian beer

Performance: Indian dancers, Bollywood Actors

Casablanca

Play it again Sam!

Recreate the classic movie with you as the star... As Bogart or Bergman you can go back to that wartime era and that famous Moroccan gin joint... Outside face the dusty heat and the bustling streets with their traders and wandering camels... Inside the cool white walls of Rick's Place take a drink at the bar and listen to the sounds of Sam at the piano... Watch who you speak to though for not everyone is what they seem and spies hide themselves in the shadows of the night...

Moody club-style Ricks Café entrance with large kentia palm trees in huge pots and customised sign. Set a white piano and a series of saxophonist statues amongst the club.

Invites: Piano Silhouette... Meet up with me...

Styling: Moroccan with Art Deco overtones, palm trees and piano

Music: Blues pianist and solo saxophonist

Drinks: Wines, beers and shorts served from mint tea glasses

Performance: Spies, bootleggers and divas

Casino

Is Lady Luck with you tonight?

Enter the heady world of the casino where money talks and everybody is listening... Try your luck at roulette, blackjack or poker in an atmosphere of glamour and style... Everyone is dressed to impress and all around are bright lights and glitter... Beautiful girls are there to serve you drinks... Your surroundings make it hard to resist the urge to gamble, everywhere you turn you see playing cards, dollar and pound symbols and shimmering 'win' and 'lose' signs; which one will you be doing?

Customise the money, use black, silver and gold as the colour scheme and bunny girls to serve the drinks. Have Blackjack and Roulette tables.

Invites: Roulette chips in a logoed green baize pouch

Styling: Glamorous; black, gold, silver

Music: Jazz, movie themed

Drinks: Champagne and wines

Performance: Showgirls, cabaret, card sharps and magicians

Cinderella

See Cinders alone in the kitchen at the hearth by the fire...
Broomstick in hand as she dreams of going to the ball... Find the pumpkin and white mice
that will be magically transformed into her carriage by her fairy godmother... Be transported
with Cinderella to the breathtaking whirl of the ballroom, a glittering world of silver and
pink... Will she meet Prince Charming and be offered the famous glass slipper...

Create the reception as the kitchen and the main room as the ballroom, have
huge silver candelabras on the tables, set them with roses and ivy. For fun use
drag ugly sisters and godmother, along with a glass slipper for all to try.

Invites: Beautiful ballroom invitation from the Palace

Styling: Luxurious elegant ballroom, drapes and columns

Music: Classical and Waltz

Drinks: Champagnes and wines

Performance: Drag ugly sisters, liveried footmen with mouse masks

Circus

The circus has come to town!
Take your seats at ringside ladies and gentlemen and enjoy all the thrills and spills of the
Circus... Bright lights and colours are all around... Clowns having fun and playing games
in the sawdust entertaining all... See beautifully decorated rearing circus horses, performing
elephants and dangerous lions in their cages, with the ringmaster controlling all the action...

A central circular stage can have ongoing acts throughout. Dress the room with statues of amazing Circus animals, use only human acts, use juggling clubs as table centres and have a meet and greet ringmaster welcoming all the guests.

Invites: Juggling club or juggling balls

Styling: Primary colour draping and animal statues, clown imagery

Music: Barrel Organ, one-man band

Drinks: Champagne and colourful cocktails with animal cocktail sticks

Performance: Circus, trapeze, stiltwalkers

Cockney

Put on your whistle and flute, get the dustbin lids, go down the apples and pears and out onto the East End streets that resound with the noise from the famous bow bells... Join the hustle and bustle of an area alive with activity and the noises of an East End community... Grab a bite to eat from the eel and pie shop and take a look at what's on offer on the market stalls where traders shout for your attention... Stop a while and enjoy a friendly welcome at a local ale house... Rest your pint on a barrel outside and watch the pearly kings and queens as they pass by...

Singing flower girls with posies for guests, set the area with a street scene, old lampposts and barrows. Use baskets of flowers on the table, rough table cloths and allow visits by known characters such as the famous Artful Dodger.

Invites: In the design of an East End pub sign

Styling: Old street scenes, market stalls, lamp posts, barrels

Music: Piano and banjo

Drinks: Ales and wines

Performance: Music hall, spoons player, pearly kings and queens, pick pockets

Colonial

Step back in time to an era when Britannia ruled the waves... Join others at the Raffles Club and be cooled from the midday sun by large pukha fans... Look out at the game reserve close by and see passing zebras and lions basking in the heat... Mounted animal heads on plaques and animal skins show off the hunters' successes... Bamboo and wicker decorate everything along with beautiful terracotta pots and kentia palms... Polo sticks and croquet sets stand resting as their owners take a break at the bar...

Ephemera, chaise lounge and pukha bearers set the scene for the club bar, colonial dressed waiters with pith helmets serve the drinks, use bamboo furniture for the tables and chairs and a wonderful jazz band to accompany the meal. Remember to use our animal friends

Invites: Pith helmet

Styling: Colonial, wicker and airy, safari, club house photos and trophies

Music: Jazz band and Military band

Drinks: Long cocktails, Singapore Sling

Performance: Old Colonels, pukha fanners, drunken game hunters

Cotton Club

Whisper the password and enter the heady world of this infamous 1920's night-spot, frequented by only the most glamorous people, and home to notorious members of the underworld... Hidden in the shadows are watchful gangsters and their beautiful molls, reminding all who run this operation what can happen to those who cross the boss... As guests enjoy forbidden pleasures inside, outside the look-out boy stands ready to warn off trouble from the FBI...

Bootleggers to meet and greet, violin cases are set on overturned barrels.
Warehouse reception with drinks served from behind bars.
Enter the Cotton Club with red-clad small tables each lit by Tiffany lamps.

Invites: Gangster guns

Styling: Red velvet swagging with moody lighting

Music: Jazz and 1920s soul singers

Drinks: Champagne, Godfather cocktails

Performance: Bootleggers, molls, and gangsters

Dockside

Follow the scent of fresh salty air as it leads you down to the docks and their lively atmosphere... Watch the boats as they come in to unload their ocean bounty... Nets burst with fish and lobster pots are full... Traders shout from their stalls to be heard amongst the hustle and bustle... Follow the signs and enjoy a drink at one of the many dockside pubs that tempt in the passers by...

Beautiful boats serving fresh prawns on sticks, fisherman clad in waterproof gear singing old sailing shanties. A fresh seafood bar serving champagne and oysters. Large fishing nets overhead filled with star fish and seaweed, gingham table cloths set on small tables and lit by tiny lights set in shells.

Invites: Starfish or crab

Styling: Cobbled dockside street scenes, fishing nets swathed in festoon lighting

Music: Shanty singers

Drinks: Beer and wines

Performance: Fishermen, Molly Malone cockle-seller girls

Dutch

Enjoy a trip to the bright and colourful country of Holland...Visit the famous tulip fields which spread an abundance of beautiful colours across the horizon... See the wonderful windmills in all styles and sizes as their sails turn in the blue skies above... Stop one of the local girls dressed in traditional Dutch costume and buy some flowers from their baskets... Try on a pair of clogs for size or sample the delicious Edam cheese on sale...

Canapés served from oversized clogs by traditional Dutch girls with blonde plaits and curled up hats. A stage decorated with oversized tulips against a huge central windmill and a background of tulip fields flanked by two beautiful windmills.

Invites: Windmill with moving sails

Styling: Windmills, tulips and bicycles with oversized clog table centres

Music: Dutch traditional and live band

Drinks: Champagne and Dutch beers

Performance: Clog dancing, flower girls and cheese rolling

Easter

Spring is in the air... All around beautiful flowers are beginning to bloom... Little lambs gambol in the green grass and tiny chicks emerge from their shells... Now is the time that kids of all ages love, time for the Easter bunny to appear with their basket full of delicious chocolate eggs for all to enjoy... Take a seat at the picnic table and tuck in!

Rabbits meet and greet. Beautiful oversized Easter games can be set in a woodland cottage setting with huge flowers, an Easter bunny and colourful toadstools. Large daffodils and baskets full of colourful hand-painted eggs. Set the tables arrangements on green slip cloths scattered with miniature candy-coated chocolate eggs.

Invites: Easter Egg with invite inside

Styling: Woodland, oversized bunnies and daffodils

Music: Band on a bandstand

Drinks: Wine and Bucks Fizz or chocolate Vodkas

Performance: Fancy dress parade and bunny characters with Easter games

Egyptian

Brave the desert heat and see for yourself one of the seven wonders of the world, the stunning pyramids that rise out of the sand... Escape from the sun under a palm tree in a desert oasis... Take a trip to a camel sale and pick yourself up a ride... Visit the Bedouin market and try to resist the traders' urges to buy their carpets or beautiful brass ware... See the amazing sphinx or the mask of Tutankhamen... Just watch out for the curse of the mummy!

Central oversized sphinx with Anubis dogs, desert backdrop flanked by a train of camels. A corner for hubbly bubblies all set on Egyptian carpets in a colourful Bedouin tent.

Invites: 3D pyramid

Styling: Gold and turquoise draping, desert palms, sphinx and pyramid backdrops

Music: Egyptian band

Drinks: Wine and mint tea

Performance: Belly dancers, soothsayers, bed of nails

Elvis

Enter a world where music is everything and the King of Rock & Roll rules... All around you see Elvis posters, guitars and musical notes... The jukebox in the diner plays non-stop hits from the King... See the legend himself in all his incarnations... Recreate the famous Jailhouse Rock scenes for yourself... Say goodbye to taste and re-live those rhinestone-clad Vegas years with glitter and bright colours everywhere, golden candelabras and a shiny red Cadillac...

Elvis statues set against a diner, Graceland's gates to enter, Rock and Roll dancers on an Elvis stage. Canapés served from guitars, and have pictures taken on the red Cadillac sofa.

Invites: Guitar or Elvis cut-out

Styling: Elvis statues, Wurlitzer and bright neons

Music: Elvis Rock and Roll

Drinks: Slush puppies, beer and wine

Performance: Elvis look-a-likes and Chinese Elvis impersonators

Fairground

Roll up! Roll up! Come and enjoy all the fun of the fair...
Follow the bright lights and they will lead you to all the action... Try your luck at all
the fun fairground games and stalls... Can you knock down a coconut to win a prize?...
Aim straight at the shooting gallery and you wont go away empty-handed... Hook
yourself a duck and bag even more booty to take home... Show off to your friends
on the test of strength game... Laugh as you see yourself in the distorting mirrors...
Amongst all the colourful stalls find delicious popcorn and candyfloss to enjoy...

Set up a fun fair, don't forget the famous dancing horses. Have clowns going around with popcorn, make each table a different bright colour. Use goldfish bowls with gifts for guests.

Invites: Fairground poster

Styling: Traditional fairground stalls, including coconut, shooting
and hoopla, distorting mirrors and carousel horses

Music: Fairground barrel organ

Drinks: Champagne and wines

Performance: Stilt walkers, jugglers, bearded ladies, gypsy crystal ball reader

Fifties

Step back in time to when the teenager was first created and Rock & Roll ruled the air waves... Hang out at the diner and grab a milkshake and a hot dog... Check where your favourite songs are on the billboard charts then put your dimes in the jukebox and jive the night away... See Buddy Holly and other 50s icons like James Dean and Marilyn Monroe... Dream of owning a pink Cadillac like the homecoming queen...

Fast-food stands and oversized pink sundaes all served from the traditional diner. Pink Cadillac sofas and a Chevrolet bar set a cool chill out area. Usherette girls dressed in cute short skirts hand out hot dogs and popcorn. Cult poses in statue form of Marilyn, James Dean and Elvis epitomise the true fifties

Invites: CD of fifties tunes printed to look like vinyl disk

Styling: Pink and chrome diner style, Marilyn and James Dean memorabilia, bubble gum machines

Music: Fifties jukebox

Drinks: Milkshakes and beer

Performance: Jive dancers and prom queens

Forties

Stand to attention everybody!

Enter a world of discipline, rules and regulations with a long and heroic history behind it... Go back in time and relive the dramatic events of the World at War... See the effects of the Blitz... Feel your adrenaline rush as the air raid siren sounds... Grab your gun and gas mask, salute Churchill, and head for the bunker!... Try an army camp bed out for size then head to the mess for your rations...

Cover the ceiling with cammo nets, use military signs throughout. Create a military mess and serve drinks from tin mugs. Have a bunker entrance and a wonderful sculpture of Churchill. Use hurricane lamps as table centres and flags as slip cloths.

Invites: Ration book

Styling: Military tones, cammo nets, Blitz backdrops, bunting, welcome home signs

Music: Big Swing or military band

Drinks: Wine and beer from tin mugs

Performance: Sgt. Major and Churchill look-alikes

Fire & Ice

Step inside a world of extremes as you enter the realms of fire and ice...

Feel the chill in the air of the ice kingdom... A world of cool blues and shimmering silvers... Ice caves stand guarded by beautiful ice maidens, and arctic creatures hide in their snowy domain as a sleigh passes through the silvery trees, twinkling with tiny lights... The heat soon rises as you step into the fiery world beyond... Reds, oranges and golds surround you as flames flicker and dance into the air...

Design a wonderful ice-effect interior in one area and reflect the fire-
side in another, dress flame-lights with icicles and reflect with hot reds.
Use glowing red and blue cubes in drinks and on tables.

Invites: Translucent pouch of glow cubes in red and white

Styling: Silver/blue and red/gold, add icy dressed flame lights and ice sculptures

Music: Classical Orchestra playing themes related to fire and ice

Drinks: Champagne, Kir Royale and wines

Performance: Fire and ice dancers and ballet performers

Formula One

Hear the roar of the engines, smell the tyres burning...

*Watch the action... feel the excitement... enter the exhilarating world of motor racing...
Take a trip to the pitstop and see the crews at work changing tyres and refuelling... After the
chequered flag drops see the winners take to the podium to open their champagne...*

Trophies for table centres, pitstop tunnel entrance, seating areas made from stacks of
tyres. Dress the staff in Formula One racing overalls, and have a Scalextric for fun.

Invites: Black and white chequered flag

Styling: Black and white, racing scenery and full and parts of race cars

Music: Racing sound effects and music from Grand Prix movie (1966)

Drinks: Champagne

Performance: Pitstop hosts with Scalextric, look-a-like race drivers,
hostesses with top up drinks served from jerry cans

Football

Here we go, here we go, here we go!

Join the crowd on the football terraces... Check the team lists... See the trophies, even the world cup, and pictures of past players... Watch out for football hooligans in the crowd... Get your scarves and flags ready to wave as the teams take to the pitch...

Surround the room with crowd backdrops, create a pitch on the ground, have football pyramids as the table centres, use table football for ongoing tournaments.

Invites: Red and yellow cards

Styling: Crowd backdrops, astro turf, flags from all nations, footballer silhouettes

Music: Popular and football anthems

Drinks: Lager

Performance: Jugglers with mini footballs, football supporters
and David Beckham look-a-like, Penalty shoot out

Fourth of July

Celebrate the anniversary of American Independence in true stateside style... Red, white and blue are all around with the stars and stripes flying proudly everywhere... Join the crowds and be tempted by the hamburgers and hot dogs on sale nearby... The American eagle, the ultimate symbol of freedom, and the Statue of Liberty, watch over the fun... As the sun goes down see the fireworks light up the night sky...

Drape the venue in red, white and blue scallops. Use a balloon drop. Dress the tables patriotically. Use a Statue of Liberty as the centre piece. Have large American Eagles set on stage either side of an impressive American flag.

Invites: American Flag

Styling: Red, white and blue colour scheme, balloons and flags

Music: Traditional American band

Drinks: Champagne and American beer

Performance: American cheerleaders, usherettes

France

Take a trip to la belle France and experience it's delights...
Stroll along Parisian streets and you can almost smell the fresh baguettes and
cheeses that hang from market stalls... Maybe stop at the onion vendor with his
bike and try his wares... See the Eiffel Tower... Visit the infamous Moulin Rouge
then take in the left bank and see the artists with their colourful palettes...

Transform the room with traditional lampposts, hanging flower baskets,
market stalls and street signs, centralise the Eiffel Tower. Set the stage as the
Moulin Rouge with Can Can girls and covers from these famous shows.

Invites: Artist's palette

Styling: French cafe scene and markets, Eiffel tower and The Moulin Rouge

Music: Accordion

Drinks: Champagne, Pastis and Kir Royal

Performance: Can Can girls, flower girls and portrait painters

German

Breath in the crisp clean mountain air... Take in all the beautiful scenery around you... Stop at the local market and be tempted by all the produce such as freshly baked bread, delicious sausages and brightly coloured flowers all displayed in rustic wooden market carts... Pass through the streets where flags and bunting brighten up the day and head for the local Bierkeller to raise a large stein of beer with friends... Skol!

Clad the room with mountain backdrops, use Bavarian street scenery for the stage, create a Bierkeller with large barrels flanking the rustic wooden bar, long tables and benches dressed in gingham. Serve the beer from steins.

Invites: Customised steins

Styling: Mountainous and Traditional street scenes

Music: Oompah band

Drinks: German Beers, Weiss beers

Performance: Lederhosen clad dancers, bell ringers

Golf

Follow the crowds down to the green to watch all the action at the international tournament or fulfil that secret ambition to put your skills to the test against the best... The sun shines down on the course as competitors tee off amidst a sea of stars and stripes flags... Will you get a hole-in-one or hit the rough... Take a break, enjoy a cold beer or a cool milkshake, and sample the delights of the many food stalls that try to tempt you as you shade under your bright golfing umbrella...

Astro turf the floor, have huge golf umbrellas for each table, use a simulated golfing tournament for guests to play, have large screens and oversized clubs and balls for the stage. Guests arrive by golf buggy. Don't forget to add crazy golf as an activity, it is both visual and fun, indoors and out.

Invites: Golf score card

Styling: Light and green, golf buggies, score boards

Music: Jazz band

Drinks: Long cocktails and Champagne

Performance: Caddy boys and girls, caricaturists with pre-set golfing pads

Grease

Join the gang at Rydell High for the last days of high school... See the T-birds and the Pink Ladies hanging out at the diner enjoying burgers and milkshakes or checking out their wheels... Visit the school as they prepare for the dance... Pink and black are the colours everywhere... Have some fun at the fairground, try your luck at the stalls and games or have a photo taken through a fun peep-through board... See the famous pink Cadillac before it takes to the skies!

Emulate the Rydell High school prom party; have fairground games around the room and a stage with a beautiful scene from Grease, encompass the T-birds and Pink Ladies. Flank the bar with large oversized milkshakes. Set up a pop-corn and candy floss stall. Use pink and black balloon arches, and give tiaras to the prom queens.

Invites: Prom invite

Styling: School prom, balloons, long tables and fairground games

Music: Grease tracks and jive

Drinks: Milkshakes, slush puppies and beer

Performance: Jivers, T-birds and Pink ladies to meet and greet

Greek

Enjoy a traditional warm, friendly Greek welcome and experience their amazing history and culture... See beautiful classic statues and columns from ancient days alongside stone urns and balustrades... Traditional Grecian busts stand proud on plinths... Head to the seashore and enjoy the delights of a sleepy Greek village... Watch the boats bring in their fresh bounty in nets and lobster pots... Visit the local taverna and enjoy a pitcher of wine but watch out for smashing plates!

Dress the room in broken classical statues, urns spilling with bougainvillea. Have spectacular table centres using different Greek statues; use Perspex chairs and table and design customised scrolls for the menus. Add a stone dance floor surrounded by balustrade. Create the reception as a taverna with colourful boats and overhead fishing nets.

Invites: Column or plate with message hand written on it

Styling: Classical stones and whites, Greek columns and statues with fresh greenery

Music: Greek traditional and Harpsichord and flute

Drinks: Traditional retsina wine and ouzo

Performance: Greek dancers and plate smashing

Heaven & Hell

Where do you belong..?

Enter the gates of Hell if you dare... Pass through the fiery entrance where devils wait to greet the damned... Darkness reigns in Satan's domain, only the light from black candles illuminate the blood red all around... Pass through the gates of Heaven and into Paradise... White clouds seem to float by... Misty lights hover in the air above..... Light sticks create an ethereal feel as pearly white candles shine light all around from earthly bowls...

Dfferent spaces different feel; drinks in Heaven, followed by dancing in Hell, on a black dance floor glowing with the devil's horns. Use floating cherubs as table centres for Heaven and light up skulls for Hell. Have a chill out area, combining the Heaven and Hell

Invites: Tombstone RSVP instead of RIP!

Styling: Pearly Gate entrance, light sticks and columns, candelabras and Satan's Bar

Music: Dramatic orchestra with famous overtures

Drinks: Blood red or glowing white cocktails, and wine

Performance: Angels statues, St. Peter and the walking dead

Highland

Take a trip to bonny Scotland...

The Scottish thistle is evident all around amongst the different clan tartans... Shields, swords and spears show the history of fighting that has troubled this land... See beautiful deer stand proud amongst the rocks of the highlands... You can almost hear the bagpipes on the wind... In the ancestral castle pennants and flags add decoration as do paintings of the castle's former inhabitants... Pewter tankards and plates sit ready for the feasting to begin...

Create long banqueting tables; add huge central candelabra and dress in tartan. Use black velvet cloths and velvet clad benches. Set the stage with highland backdrops flanked by golden thistles. Use 3ft platters and a piper to pipe in the haggis.

Invites: Tartan invite with a sprig of heather

Styling: Scottish baronial, tartans and candelabra, wrought iron candelabra

Music: Bagpipes

Drinks: Mead, wine and hot Scotch toddies

Performance: Scottish dancers, storytellers and Robert Burns poems

Hollywood

Lights, camera, action!

Tonight you're the star in the glitzy world of Hollywood... Tell the paparazzi 'no comment' as they clamour to take your picture and get the best quotes... Mingle with film stars from past and present in an atmosphere of style and glamour... Greta Garbo, Charlie Chaplin and John Wayne all make a special appearance... Make a dream come true and receive your very own award or take a seat in your director's chair and control all the action...

Red carpet treatment, decorate the room with elegant huge kentia palms, Hollywood awards and statues of famous characters such as Schwarzenegger, Bogart and Marlon Brando. Use film-can table centres, black cloths and starlets for drinks service.

Invites: Mini Award statues

Styling: Elegant, gold and black overall, clapper boards, movie cameras and awards

Music: Movie theme covers band

Drinks: Champagne and wine

Performance: Starlets, paparazzi, film directors

Hong Kong

Explore the delights of this city of contrasting cultures...

Dominated by a skyline of skyscrapers the city still retains its ancient roots... Traditional rickshaws travel the roads alongside cars... The streets are alive with bustling markets with lively traders vying for your attention and your money... Beautiful oriental banners and fans are used for decoration everywhere and their sumptuous colours are picked up in the silks and flowers for sale... You can almost smell the delicious food served from street side carts...

Fans and good luck pennants set amongst rickshaws and neons. Tables laid in stark white cloths with traditional rice-inlaid crockery. Use Lazy Susans for starters and Chinese acrobats for entertainment. Do not forget the huge imposing dragon, with glowing eyes welcoming the guests.

Invites: Fan with good luck script

Styling: Red, black gold and bamboo, with neons, giant fans and gold statues

Music: Chinese traditional

Drinks: Sake, Champagne and Mai Tai

Performance: Chinese acrobats and coolies

Indiana Jones

Through the deserts of the Sahara to steamy jungles and snowy expanses, do battle with the forces of evil and greed... Hunt for the Lost Ark yourself before the deadly Nazis get their hands on it... Cut through vines to find gods hidden in secret passages... Encounter animals in the wild, some are friendly but some are not! Join Indy in the pursuit for hidden treasure all over the world...

Mix the stories together or choose one. Hanging vines and a huge visage of Tutankhamen on stage, enter through flaming boulders into the jungle area with monkeys, snakes, fearsome wooden carvings and scripted stone tablets. Dress the staff in leather jerkins, give the guests whips to play with. Table centres can be chests filled with golden coins. Have life size mannequin of him in person centred by a massive stack of books and urns.

Invites: Treasure map

Styling: Archaeological statues, jungle and greenery, boulders and ferocious animal statues

Music: Movie soundtrack and Arabic band

Drinks: Champagne and wine

Performance: Characters from movie, Whip Cracker, snake charmer

Journey to the Centre of the Earth

Journey to the centre of the earth and touch the primeval fires which stir in the world's belly... Giant flames encompass and illuminate the entrance, whilst small flames jump from the blaze and trip through the main room... In the distance the blistering sun sears down on diners and issue forth the changing seasons throughout the setting... Each table erupts with smouldering light which weaves through the volcanic depths... Swathes of crimson and gold burn through the surroundings encapsulating the room with a fiery ambience...

Use flame lights throughout, dressed in crimsons and gold, backdrops of flames, table centres with glowing minerals and smouldering rocks. Dance floor with oversized golden suns on the corners, dancing flame projections reflecting on the walls, and canapés served off slate.

Invites: A mineral and crystal-filled pouch

Styling: Moving flame projections and flaming boulders, smoke machines

Music: Electric string quartet

Drinks: Tequila Sunrise and Champagne

Performance: Aerial silk performers, fire nymphs

Italian

Mama Mia! Enjoy a little taste of Italy and experience La Dolce Vita for yourself...

Everywhere you turn see the colours of Italy, red, white and green... Wander through Italian streets and you can almost smell the delicious aroma of cheeses and salami that hang from nearby shops, tempting passers-by... Stop and sample some chianti or a little pasta then visit the gelateria... Take in the sights and sounds of Italy... See the Leaning Tower of Pisa... Beautiful gondolas and their gondoliers... Viva Italia!

Colourful green, red and white balloons throughout, table centres of Chianti bottles with red candles set on gingham slip cloths, waiters dressed as gondoliers, serving drinks from gondolas. Beautiful Roman statues, fountains and broken vases add to the ambience.

Invites: Musical sheet

Styling: Leaning Tower of Pizza, piazza-style furniture and gondola food stations

Music: Italian traditional choir, such as Coro Care Alto

Drinks: Asti Spumante and Chianti

Performance: Opera singers dressed as gondoliers and Gladiators

James bond

The name's Bond, James Bond...

Welcome to the world of 007, a heady mix of intrigue and glamour, of secret agents, evil villains and beautiful women... Guests enter through a stunning entrance leading to Moneypenny's office, they later visit Q's laboratory to see what delights lie inside... Walking upon a luxury red carpet flanked by gold stanchions and rope, guests pass elegant kentia palms, flambeaux, Bond silhouettes, and glittering Bond signs to make their way to all the action...

Superb theme for action and participation from around the world, ideal for black tie parties. Bond look-a-likes meet and greet, casino runs after dinner, tables are set elegantly on black cloths and mirror bases. Games include shooting, and simulators.

Invites: Gold Bondesque silhouette of the host

Styling: Luxurious add action backdrops, giant martini glass table centres, Octopussy aeroplane

Music: Cover band with female soloist performing classic Bond tracks

Drinks: Champagne and Martinis

Performance: Dancing Bond girls behind screens, Gold Bond girl living statues

Jazz

After hours in the city knock on the door of a side alley building and enter the dark and smoke-filled world of the jazz club... On stage the lady sings the blues as the boys in the band play along... The black and white dance floor fills with slow moving couples... Through the hazy air shine the bright lights of the neon signs pointing the way to the bar, where guys sit with their drinks nursing broken hearts, waiting for Lady Luck to show up... The walls are lined with pictures of all the jazz legends and shimmering notes hang all around...

Neon-lit street scene stage dressed with deep purple drapes, long, wooden bar set with musical ephemera. Jazz musician statues set around the room. Black and white dance floor.

Invites: Saxophone-shaped invite

Styling: Jazz club, neon lights, velvet drapes and starcloths

Music: Jazz and blues

Drinks: Champagne and cocktails

Performance: Singers and hostesses in slinky dresses, cigar girls and bouncers,

Jungle

Take a trip into the heart of the jungle... Amongst the lush greenery grow exotic flowers that bring colour and beauty to the darker corners... The warm, moist air is filled with sound of birds that fly overhead and the animals that live in the trees as well as those that roam free on the ground... The monkeys howl as the guests arrive and greet them with bright delight... Thick vines hang down from the canopy of trees and if you are lucky you may see Tarzan himself as he swings past... Follow him to his tree house and see Jane who waits for him there...

Fabulous 5ft palm trees on tables, backdrops of the jungle with beautiful huge parrots on perches throughout. Chairs wrapped with vines, dance floor dressed under a jungle canopy.

Invites: Bug in a walnut

Styling: Tarzan Tree house jungle bar, animal print seating, hanging greenery

Music: Jungle drummers

Drinks: Champagne and fresh jungle juice cocktails from bamboo glass holders

Performance: Loin-clothed Tarzan and Jane contortionists, static acrobats on vine-clad trapeze

Jurassic Park

Take a visit to the ultimate theme park... But will you get out alive?
See the scientists at work in their hi-tech laboratory recreating the creatures that roamed the Earth
millions of years before man existed... If you dare then explore the island jungle... Fight your way
through the dense greenery that surrounds you... Watch out for indigenous animals that lurk
in the foliage but most importantly try and avoid the creatures who have been allowed to roam
here, whose yellow eyes stare out from the dark, especially whoever made that huge footprint!

Huge dinosaurs set in jungle vines, rock-effect dance floor with large nests of oversized dinosaur eggs. Tables with dinosaur heads protruding from their centre. Stage set with two prehistoric cavemen against jungle scenery.

Invites: Dinosaur bone

Styling: Dinosaur statues, intense greenery, flame lights from jungle boulders, fairy firefly lights, dinosaur bones, Jurassic juice bar

Music: Flintstone Rock-inspired band

Drinks: Spirits on the glowing rocks

Performance: Cavemen and cave girls, rope trick magicians, Jurassic photo area

Las Vegas

Viva Las Vegas! This is not a place for subtlety... Here everything is big and bright... Glitzy and glamourous or tacky and tasteless... Anyone can be a winner here, you can walk in with nothing and leave like a King... Gold and silver shine all around you tempting you in to try your luck at the tables... Beautiful showgirls entertain you while you take a break... Once you enter this world you may never be able to leave!

Chips and customised money on tables for guests for usc in the casino and on the Wheel of Fortune. The Strip decor for the room, beautiful palm trees in golden pots and with dice as tables throughout. Tables dressed with magnificent glass and gold candelabras. Tryout a Chapel of Love with Elvis taking your vows..

Invites: Customised oversized dollar bill

Styling: Luxurious, gold and pink, with flamingoes and neons, giant dice against playing card backdrops, showgirl silhouettes and the Chapel of Love

Music: American showstoppers

Drinks: Champagne cocktails

Performance: Showgirls, Rat Pack look-a-likes

Masked Ball

As night falls an air of mystery descends over all... Flames from the candles of beautiful candelabras flicker and dance spreading soft light all around... Behind fluted columns hide beautiful strangers, their true identities hidden by stunning masks... Giant comedy/tragedy figures smile and frown at passing guests... Elegant feather displays adorn a room draped in reds and golds, softly lit to enhance the enigmatic atmosphere... Harlequin statues seem to dance to the music that floats through the air.

Tables are dressed with rich gold lame covers. Feather displays incorporating comedy and tragedy masks or exquisite carnival masks make the table centre. Elegant draping is offset by beautiful candelabra. Comedia Del'Arte inspired statues adorn the room amongst huge gold frames and swirl topped columns.

Invites: Mask

Styling: Giant masks, flambeaux swathed in feathers, dancer statuettes, feather displays, ornate columns, and oversized mirrors

Music: Venetian Orchestral music

Drinks: Champagne

Performance: Liveried footmen and Comedia Del'Arte

Medieval

Cross through the drawbridge entrance and enter a bygone era... Be transported to a world of knights in armour who fight to defend the honour of beautiful damsels, of dark dungeons awaiting traitors and blaggards... Mirth and merriment abound, with hearty enjoyment of food and drink and the finest entertainers in the kingdom performing for the people's pleasure...

Create a dungeon reception. Invite a Lord Chamberlain to do a ceremony for the for the feast, use stocks and pillories, have the mead served from ceramic jugs and poured into pewter goblets by buxom wenches. Create a magnificent banquet with pennant slips and velvet cloths set on long tables adorned with magnificent platters of food. Use benches and balloons to add a jovial atmosphere for Jesters to play.

Invites: King's ransom scroll

Styling: Medieval Banquet, suits of armour, hanging pennants, pewter, settings, medieval thrones, stocks, racks and pillories

Music: Strolling Medieval minstrels

Drinks: Mead, cider and wine

Performance: Jousting knights, serving wenches, jesters

Mexican

Arriba! Arriba! Round up your amigos and join the Fiesta!

Cactii and chillies are abundant under the desert sun... Escape the heat and head down to the cantina... Enjoy a tequila served by one of the local senoritas but watch out for banditos dozing under their sombreros... Party the night away to the sounds of Mexican musicians that fill the warm evening air...

Design the cantina with trestle tables and benches covered in colourful slip cloths, have an entrance of corral fencing and cacti and meet and greet Mexicans. Serve Tex Mex food and tequilas all night.

Invites: Chilli pepper

Styling: Cantina, cactii, ponchos slung over corral fencing against desert backdrops, South American figures and sequined sombreros

Music: Mariachi and Mexican traditional band

Drinks: Tequila and cocktails including Mexican Ruin and Sombreros

Performance: Tequila girls and Mexican banditos

Midsummer Night's Dream

Dancing and frolicking among sparkling pathways...

*As dusk falls... the beautiful and mystical world of the fairies awaits the
arriving guests... for an enchanting and magical evening...
A spectacular scene... as the inhabitants of the woodland come out to play, amongst
amazing settings with oversized toadstools and huge twinkling trees...*

Make a magical entrance, have a fairy swinging on an ivy clad rope swing, use small lights
throughout the venue, incorporate them into the table centres and all decorations. Use
forest colour cloths and sprinkle tea-lights amongst leaves at the base of table centres.

Invites: Fairy wings

Styling: Magical woodland, water features, toadstools and tree-
stump seating, giant flowers, and huge glittering butterflies

Music: Harp and flute

Drinks: Champagne and Absinth

Performance: Acrobats, Shakespearean actors and fairies trapeze

Nautical

Anchors away! Come aboard ship as we set sail across the seas... Stroll along the ships deck, lean over the railings and enjoy the fresh sea air... If you look closely you may spot dolphins playing in the waves... Follow signs to the front of the ship where you can take a turn at the wheel and sound the ship's bell... As the sun sets on the horizon go below deck where you can enjoy your evening's entertainment and still look out at the sea view through the portholes...

Dress the room as the ship's deck. Use logoed floatation devices, portholes, sunset backdrop, ship's bells as table centres on blue and white nautical tablecloths, and meet and greet Captains and young sailor boys in bell bottoms. Dress chairs in white with royal blue sash.

Invites: Message in a bottle

Styling: Nautical seascapes, boat funnels, ships wheels and railings, floatation devices, treasure chests, galleon backdrops and seascapes

Music: Naval band and shanties

Drinks: Rum and champagne, Sea breeze and Salty Dog

Performance: Sailors and ships captain, Hornpipe dancers, Deck coits

Olde Englande

Step back in time to the foggy streets of London town... Walk along bustling streets past market stalls that burst with their wares... Warm yourself with hot potatoes or chestnuts from the vendors nearby... See street urchins chase the penny farthings that come past... Stop by the pub and rest your beer upon a barrel outside as you watch the ladies and gentlemen in their finery pass by...

Use signage from the back streets and alleyways, visit Baker Street and the East End. Dolphin lamps at the Embankment and backdrops depicting notorious and infamous characters, Guy Fawkes and Sherlock Holmes. Set the venue with barrels and tea chests, have a period Potato oven with mini baked potatoes on sticks.

Invites: Bag of old pennies

Styling: Street scenes and traders carts, penny farthings, barels, old fashioned lamp lights, signage, sacks, ropes, and horse and cart

Music: Music Hall, Sing-along pianist

Drinks: Beer, wine, mead

Performance: Singing flower girls, Pick pockets and traders, Sherlock Holmes

Irish pub

Visit the Emerald Isle and enjoy the warm, friendly atmosphere of the local tavern...
Enter a traditional bar with wooden tables and seating... Barrels provide an extra place to rest your
pint and hay bales are somewhere else to rest your weary feet... In the heart of the country baskets,
milk churns and saddlery are common sights... Signs point the way for travellers to the bright
lights of the big cities of Dublin and Cork... Watch out for any leprechauns who may be hiding!

Use a mix of rural and traditional, set a country-style entrance with full sized cow and
sheep statues along a grassy verge. Use baskets filled with flowers and pints of Guinness
for table centres. Have a dance show Riverdance style followed by participation for guests.
Consider a solo Irish fiddler in an Irish pub, dressed in green waistcoat and breeches.

Invites: Shamrocks

Styling: Countryside and rustic with farm animals, milestones and
bunting, oversized Guinness glasses, Irish pub with wooden bar

Music: Irish traditional band with fiddler

Drinks: Guinness and poitin

Performance: Irish singers 'Danny Boy', dancers, bar skittle, pugilists and test of strength

Olympics

Be a part of the ultimate sporting contest, where nation faces nation in a fight to be the best in the world... See the famous Olympic torch burning brightly, as a historic symbol of this ancient tradition... The flags from all the countries fly proudly for all to see... Join the crowds of spectators who watch each event, cheering the battling athletes on... And keep an eye on the scoreboard to see who will be victorious and take home the gold medal...

Can be themed to the place of the original or forthcoming Olympics, if original use more classical Greek elements such as columns, urns and statues. Dress the room with a series of huge Olympic rings and use flaming torches. For tables use trophies for the various sports and Olympic flags as slip cloths. Have Sports models and large billboards with details of the events.

Invites: Gold Medal

Styling: Colourful stadium, flags, sports statues, Olympic flame lights, Grecian statues, columns and urns

Music: Orchestra for around the world anthems

Drinks: Champagne and wine

Performance: Live statues holding Olympic flames, acrobats and trainers

Orient Express

Treat yourself to the trip of a lifetime on the famous Orient Express... The city of London flies by as you begin your journey to destinations such as Paris and the Far East... Sit back in luxurious surroundings, listen to the piano player at the bar, as stunning scenery passes by your window... At each stop you make enjoy the warm welcome from the locals and experience the delights of the different cultures you encounter...

This can reflect the varying countries that the train stops at. Use the class and elegance of the Orient Express for the general décor. Kentia palm trees and Tiffany lamps dress the entrance, whilst the bell boys watch over the stacks of luggage. Use iconic decorations from around the world, magnificent dragons, the Eiffel Tower, 6ft elephants and Venetian Masks. Theme the food and tables to these countries.

Invites: Boarding card

Styling: Train, luggage, Tiffany lamps, backdrops and recognised items reflecting the destinations, giant luggage labels

Music: Piano player, traditional music from destinations

Drinks: Champagne and wine

Performance: Bell boys, porters and typical ethnic characters

Oriental

Explore the mysteries of the Orient... Enjoy the sights and sounds of the bazaar where locals try to tempt you with their goods... See their displays and Buddhas from the temples... Hear the sound of chimes making music in the wind... The scent of jasmine fills the air... Pass by pagodas and decorated parasols and see colourful statues of gods... Tatami Screens are all around and a giant panda watches over everything...

Mix the Orient or choose any country. Most Oriental countries reflect colour, intricate art, lovely Kimonos and sarongs, as well as unusual wheeled transportation. Tatami screens, colourful freestanding umbrellas and pagoda arches make beautiful entrances. Create a traditional Oriental garden set with a good luck pool, beautiful hand carved Buddhas work as a background for traditional musicians.

Invites: Silk route parchment in wooden box

Styling: Tatami screens, giant gongs, water pools and features,
bamboo, bonsai trees, Buddhas and pagodas

Music: Gamalan Orchestra, Taiko Drummers

Drinks: Sake and wines and jasmine tea

Performance: Oriental acrobats and oriental bookmarks, silhouette cutters, sumo wrestlers

Pantomime

As the red curtains open step through a giant storybook and onto the stage... Recreate your favourite panto, complete with ugly pantomime dames who are bound to cause trouble... You could be Cinders, sat in front of the fire dreaming of going to the ball and meeting Prince Charming... Have a go at rubbing Aladdin's lamp and see the giant genie appear to grant you three wishes... Join Dick Whittington and his cat on the road to London to find his fortune or see Ali Baba and the forty thieves hidden in their pots...

This can be a varied scheme or set as particular theme. The room is set as the stage, drapes throughout and wonderful live tableaux sets from pantos. Each table a different panto with an accompanying poster on a crushed velvet cloth and mirrored base.

Invites: Theatre programme

Styling: Stage velvet drapes and backdrops Panto silhouettes, tables individually themed

Music: Orchestra with pantomime songs

Drinks: Wines and beers

Performance: Panto MC "oh no she isn't" drag characters, and principle boys

Pirates

Enter if you dare the secret island lair of the pirates... Dark and dangerous from the outside, only the bravest seafarers dare enter to search for the treasure hidden within... The sight of the skull and crossbones flags that loom overhead act as a warning not to try... but the lure of the pirate's gold is just too strong...

Skeletons dressed in pirate's clothing, huge ship's wheels and anchors, a stage dressed with a wonderful galleon and overflowing treasure chests. Dress the tables with hurricane lamps on rough hemp, drinks served from old rum jars by the infamous pirates of the Caribbean... Gifts for guests from loot sacks scattered amidst the lamps each with golden chocolate coins and pearls cascading out.

Invites: Treasure chest with Pirate map

Styling: Pirates and flags, ships wheels and anchors, treasure chests and barrels

Music: Roving pirate fiddlers and accordion players

Drinks: Rum cocktails

Performance: Pirate pickpockets, swashbucklers with sword displays

Prehistoric

Travel back to the dawn of time to a terrifying world before man ruled the Earth, where dinosaurs were the masters and battles for survival were fought everyday... The landscape is barren but beautiful, rocky formations created by the unpredictable forces of nature... Cavemen in their furs and skins hide in their caves as they hear the sounds of dinosaurs approaching... Will it be a friendly creature or the ferocious T-rex?

Make a cave entrance. The tables are set with prehistoric salt formations, dinosaurs and semi-precious stones. Hessian cloths strewn with particles of sand and salt are lit by twinkling candles set in rocks. Stone pillars with erupting flames glowing in the misty depth of the forest, hanging vines hold snakes which hiss as you pass.

Invites: Miniature dinosaur egg

Styling: Lava formations, stone statues, minerals, dinosaur lairs, prehistoric animal skins, flaming pillars

Music: Dinosaur special effects, primitive drums

Drinks: Caveman Cocktails in frozen salty rimmed glasses

Performance: Cave painters and caricaturists

Riverboat

Through the warm southern night air you can hear the sounds that come from the Riverboat, tempting you to come and sample all the fun that waits aboard... Lively jazz music mingles with laughter and chatter... Try and hold onto your dollars as you pass the gaming tables... Stop at the bar for a drink and watch the dancing girls perform... As you leave in the early hours of the morning take care not to fall in the water or the crocs of the Mississippi will get you!

Mark Twain and Boy Friday meet your guests. The gambling takes place on board, with a fabulous set of jazz players set around the room and small tables set with green baize for dinner. Use verandah backdrops with window boxes filled with flowers for the stage and a set of huge funnels. Tiffany lamps and black and white furniture adorn the space.

Invites: Paddle wheel

Styling: Ship's funnels, kentia palms, verandah backdrops and river boat scenes, jazz musician paintings and monotone furniture

Music: Deep South Jazz

Drinks: Rum Cocktails and wines

Performance: Saloon girls, tap dancers and casino

Robin Hood

Ride through the glen with Robin Hood and his merry band of men... Cross over the drawbridge entrance and enter evil King John's feasting hall adorned with shields and armour from past battles... Later take a turn outside the castle walls where Sherwood Forest evokes a world of honourable bandits stealing from the rich to give to the poor... Relax with Friar Tuck and Maid Marian around the camp fire where mirth and merriment abound with hearty enjoyment of food and drink

Met by Robin Hood the Sherwood Forest entrance leads the way to the castle, heraldic flags, royal pennants and flaming torches set the scene for the banquet. Crushed velvet burgundy cloths and organza runners clad with huge candelabras. Each guest receives their pouch of golden coins at the place they will sit.

Invites: Bow and arrow

Styling: Forest backdrops, shields, pennants, candelabra, bows and arrows, men in armour, earthenware platters and knives made from bone

Music: Medieval band of merry men

Drinks: Mead and wine

Performance: King John MC, Robin Hood and his merry men jesters

Roman

*Go back in time to an age when the mighty Roman Empire stretched far across the world...
Experience life as a wealthy inhabitant of the city of Rome... Lie back as a servant fans you and
feeds you grapes in your magnificent home, full of classical columns and busts, beautiful vases and
statues.... Experience the life of the masses as you pass through bustling markets where traders vie
for your attention... Look out for the centurions on watch or you could end up facing the lions!*

Rose petals paving the way, through muslin drapes, stunning classical busts
and columns dressed with vines and ivy, matching dance floor with balustrade
and golden lions set on plinths. Tables set with cascading urns full of ripe
grapes, while singing nymphs strum the lute in a rose-strewn pool.

Invites: Laurel wreaths

Styling: Classical white and gold drapes, busts, vases and statues,
chariot centrepiece, Roman games and market place

Music: Roman trumpeters and lute players

Drinks: Champagne red wines and grape juice

Performance: Centurions with standards, Gladiators, and wine carriers

Safari

Listen to the call of the wild... Enjoy a once in a lifetime trip to see fabulous animals in their natural environment... Through your binoculars see if you can spot anything on the horizon... Get in closer to see majestic elephants move sedately past... Zebra with their distinctive colourings stand out against the subdued colours of the plains... Just keep an eye on the wary rhino who watches you intently...

Be greeted by families of zebra, packs of lions, screeching apes and pink flamingoes, all set against a safari background. Bamboo shacks dressed with palm leaves make a stopover for a quick cool beer. Tables dressed in faux animal skins, centre pieces of palm trees canopies, and others with parrots on their perch reflect the delights of the bush.

Invites: Mini camera

Styling: Hessian drapes and backdrops of African plains, big game statues, safari jeep seating

Music: African bongos

Drinks: Champagne and coconut cocktails

Performance: Safari guides, acrobatic animal contortionists, flame throwers

Sixties

The Beatles take the world by storm, all hip and happening London is the place to be, check out Carnaby street for yourself... Bright psychedelic colours or simple black and white are hot... Skirts are short and the make up heavy... Make your own peace protest... Check out where your favourite band is in the charts... Put their latest hit on the jukebox and twist the night away...

Enter over the Abbey Road zebra crossing with fans cheering and set with silhouettes of the Beatles. Use the jukebox in reception playing only 60's classics. Black and white Mary Quant-influenced cloths on the tables with funky colourful furniture for the cool trendy affair. Let Chubby Checker play the twist to the rocking cover band.

Invites: Ban the Bomb invite

Styling: Colourful decorations, Beatles ephemera, Abbey Road scenes

Music: Sixties Cover band

Drinks: Wine and beer

Performance: Beatles look-a-likes, twisting girls, hippy meet and greet

Seventies

Abba can be heard playing in the background as disco divas dance the night away... Guests enter into a world of platform boots, bell-bottom flares and revealing mini skirts that so epitomize the infamous decade... Travolta can be seen performing his routines on the dance floor... Glitter covered walls and neon lights draw the intrepid swingers back to a time when hair was worn long and side-burns big...

Walk through a brightly beaded entrance set with flashing dance floor panels. View a backdrop of Abba. Use psychedelic balloons and rotating mirror balls on the tables. Create a circular bar and dress with mind bending circles. Oversized vinyl 70s albums are Top of the Pops. Give wigs and funky specs to all your guests.

Invites: Mini platform boot

Styling: Giant, raised platform boots, beaded curtains, lava lamps

Music: Abba tribute band

Drinks: Psychedelic cocktails

Performance: Disco Divas meet and greet, podium disco dancers flower power tattoos

Switzerland

Head for the slopes... Enjoy the beautiful mountain scenery all around... See reindeer amongst the fir trees... Snow glistens in the sunlight... Take off your skis and your snow shoes and enjoy a little après-ski in the Winter Wonderland that Switzerland truly is... As the sun goes down tiny lights twinkle everywhere... It's time to head for the bar...

Create a winter wonderland, have a mountain hut entrance, serve gluwein out of steins. Dress the room with snow clad trees and use period skis and traditional toboggans against glorious mountain backdrops. The bar is dressed with trophies and pine wreaths. The staff serve in ski suits. The tables are old wood, the thick scented candles add a warming glow.

Invites: Ski pass

Styling: Winter chalet, fir trees, snowy backgrounds, chalet bar, animal heads

Music: Flugel Horn players, Yodellers

Drinks: Gluwein and beer from steins

Performance: Bell ringers, meet and greet chalet schnapps girls, ski simulators

Spanish

Stroll through sun drenched Spanish streets with your amigos and enjoy the history and culture of this fiery and passionate nation... Rest at the local Tapas Bar and enjoy some sangria... See sultry flamenco dancers and their beautiful Spanish fans on display... Watch the proud matadors as they show off their skills, just look out for the bull!

A huge bulls head for the entrance with colourful swags set to the sides. Dress the tables in fiery reds, have central huge floral displays decorated with matadors picks. Create a Tapas Bar and serve sangria from colourful ceramic jugs, use huge fans, Spanish dancer silhouettes and terracotta pots to dress the room.

Invites: Castanets

Styling: Hot reds with black touches, Tapas Bar scenery, hand-painted crockery, flamenco and toro silhouettes

Music: Flamenco and Gypsy Kings

Drinks: Sangria, Vino Sol and Frozen Matador cocktails

Performance: Flamenco dancers, Spanish guitarists and toreadors

Star Trek

Join the crew of the Starship Enterprise on their mission to boldly go where no man has gone before and explore space, the final frontier... Stars shine all around you as you travel the universe... On board follow the signs to the bridge and see Captain Kirk in action or be beamed down to check out an alien planet for signs of life... Always keep an eye out for Klingons!

Special sound effects, a walk through the captain's deck to have a photo opportunity in Captain Kirk chair. Dress the room with stars, meteorites and planets, use black cloths on all the tables and elevated rotating planets. Pin spot the tables, use a large space backdrop with the space ships flanked by twinkling star cloth all around the room.

Invites: Sign of the Vulcan invite

Styling: Space Scenes, star cloths, laser effects, suspended planets and meteorites, robots and alien life forms models

Music: New-age electronic orchestra

Drinks: Galactic cocktails

Performance: Star Trek characters, Klingons and Mr. Spock

Star Wars

Join Luke, Hans Solo and Princess Leia in the fight to defend the Universe from Darth Vader... Enter a space age world where the planet Earth seems light years away... Planets circle around you... Follow signs to the Cyber Space Café and take a break with all manner of alien beings... R2-D2 is at your side to help in your adventures...

Meet Princess Leia at the entrance to accompany your guests to the various Star Wars locations. Have an amazing Cyber Café with performers as the odd space bar characters, dress the stage as Tatooine, use sand nets and oil drums. Make the tables stunning by setting illuminated light rods into them and dressing with Storm Trooper masks. Use glowing square glass containers set on UV reactive cloths.

Invites: Light sabres

Styling: Alien statues, alien heads in cases, film character silhouettes, defined film set areas, jungle space and desert backdrops

Music: Alien funk band

Drinks: Margaritas with glowing cubes

Performance: Obi Wan Kenobi for magical tricks, Darth Vader for pictures, and magicians

Stock Exchange

In the heart of the capital city find the fast-paced, adrenaline-fuelled world of the Stock Exchange... Around you are all the famous sights and sounds of London but all that matters here is money, money, money... See the history of the stock market displayed on posters and cuttings from old newspapers that tell of historic market events...

Dress the reception as Jonathan's coffee shop, with street scenes and with the characters from the early days of the Stock Exchange. Use the main area as the Stock Exchange floor; have catering staff in brightly coloured blazers and use huge backdrops of the city displayed around. Dress the tables with glittering pound signs and lay the tables with blue cloths emblazoned with pound signs.

Invites: Early Trading Bond

Styling: 18th Century Jonathan's cafe and modern city trading
floor depicting share values around the world

Music: Band playing money influenced tunes

Drinks: Champagne

Performance: 18th Century money makers mixing with present day performers

Superheroes

Join your favourite superheroes in the eternal fight of good against evil... Watch the New York skyline for a glimpse of Superman flying through the air or Spiderman scaling the buildings... Enter the dark realms of Gotham City where Batman and Robin do battle against the enemies of freedom, if you look in the shadows you may catch a glimpse of Catwoman as well... See the angry incarnation of Dr. Banner, the mighty Incredible Hulk and keep a look out for the amazing Captain Marvel...

Have Spiderman swaying from a scaffold, and a Catwoman contortionist, use original cartoon style cutouts, to dress the room, add logo boards with Kapow!, Bash! and Kersplat! Incorporate a Gotham City backdrop and neon signs flanking the stage. Dress each table to a different hero, all in colours matching the pages from the original cartoons and add customised centre pieces.

Invites: Cartoon speech bubble

Styling: Superhero cutouts, Comic book-cover time tunnel,
PVC wrapped panels with giant speech bubbles

Music: Big Band playing theme tunes

Drinks: Cocktails in bright colours in logoed glasses

Performance: PVC-clad Catwoman with whip, contortionist in box, Riddler magician

The Wizard of Oz

Join Dorothy in her adventures when she takes a trip to the magical world of Oz... Follow the Yellow Brick Road and the signs for Oz as you search for the wizard himself... Along the way meet friends like the Lion, the Scarecrow and the Tin Man as they journey to find courage, a brain and a heart for themselves.... Watch out for enemies like the Wicked Witch of the West and her evil monkeys, she will be watching you in her crystal ball... Try not to fall asleep in the fields of beautiful giant flowers... When you reach Oz just click your magic slippers together and say "there's no place like home"...

Create a wonderful Yellow Brick Road as the entrance; wind it through the venue and onto the dance floor. Use long tables with centres pieces of the Emerald City and the Wicked Witch of the West. Hang coloured drapes, a background of huge flowers and trees with shining apples.

Invites: Yellow foam brick

Styling: Rainbow drapes and forest scenery, painted backdrops, witch, apple trees, farmyard animals and tools, haystacks

Music: Classic sound track, Judy Garland singer

Drinks: Emerald and Ruby cocktails with the rims of the glasses in matching coloured sugar

Performance: Scarecrow and Cowardly Lion meet and greets and Dorothy dancers

Titanic

*Take a trip back in time as you experience for yourself the timeless story of the Titanic...
Recreate some of the magical romance of the two young lovers... See life from both sides
as you enjoy the warm hospitality and lively entertainment of the third class passengers...
Drink and dance the night away to traditional Irish music amongst the spit and
sawdust... Once on the top deck you will experience the elegance and glamour of the first
class guests in an atmosphere of wealth and power... Just watch out for icebergs!*

Enter along a gangplank. Serve canapés from a life boat, dress the main area decadently with gold candelabra and wonderful art deco statues. Recreate the lower deck, have Irish music and dancers for participation. Set against ice scenery with icebergs flanking the moonlight-blue starcloth.

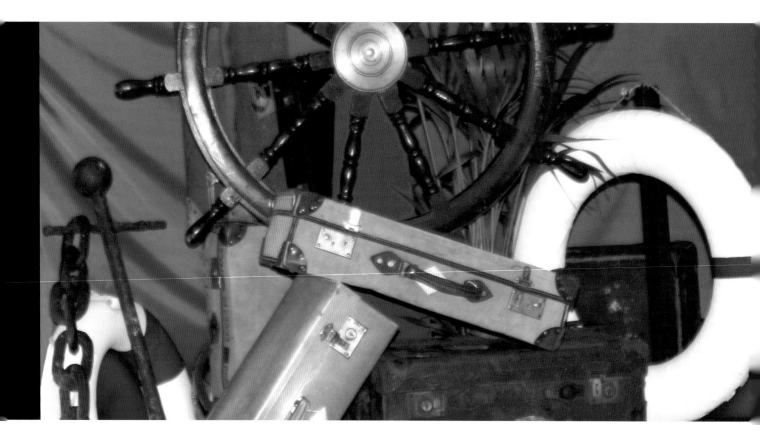

Invites: Mini suitcase with luggage tag

Styling: Split into steerage and upper class, stacks of luggage and
suspended lifeboat, icebergs, chandeliers and gold cutlery

Music: Fiddlers and Jazz band

Drinks: Champagne, wine and beers

Performance: Ships captain, Irish dancers

Tropical

Relax and enjoy the laid-back Tropical way of life... See the brightly coloured parrots perched in the surrounding palm trees... Lobsters, fish and crabs fill the fishing nets on the shore and beautiful shells lie all around... Stop at the beach bar for a cool refreshing drink before dancing to the sounds of the steel band that fill the warm night air...

Dress the room with palm trees and create a beach bar from bamboo, use more bamboo to surround the dance floor, create a beach on the stage, have palm trees with festoon lights strung across. Catering staff should be in brightly decorated shirts and tatty straw hats. Use stunning 5ft palm trees on all the tables, and add twinkling lights to set the mood. Use a steel band throughout, incorporate a limbo dancer and have a competition.

Invites: Palm Tree silhouette

Styling: Colourful tropical, palm trees, fishing nets, parrots, bamboo beach huts and bar, giant fish and floral decorations

Music: Steel band

Drinks: Blue Lagoon Cocktails and beer

Performance: Limbo, Hula girls

Underwater

Take a trip to the watery kingdom of the deep... Far below the surface of the sea is a mysterious world man rarely visits... Anchors and ship's wheels lie strewn across the sea bed... If you are lucky you may spot a lost treasure chest bursting with its bounty before the diver who searches for it... Lobsters and crabs try to avoid the nets and pots that aim to trap them... Beautiful sea horses pass sedately by and an occasional shark swims into view... If you are really lucky you may even see Neptune himself!

Create a tunnel from hanging seaweed dangling from a net adorned with sea life, a gentle wind machine and sea scent machine add special effects. Oversized statues of lobsters, sharks and sea horses set against underwater scenes. Use beautiful mermen on the corner of the dance floor, and lobster pots for the table centres brimming with fruits all entwined in an iridescent net set on a silver table cloth.

Style of invitation: Treasure chest with chocolate coins

Styling: Fishy, sea horses, mermen, and treasure chests, underwater backdrops

Music: Orchestra

Drinks: Champagne wines and beer

Performance: Fish live statues, meet and greet Neptune

Valentine

Enter a lover's paradise, a world of pinks, reds and dashes of silver... All around are love hearts and ruby red lips... A neon sign shines out 'I love you'... Cupids float above with their bows ready to shoot arrows straight to the heart... Rest on a fluffy pink sofa or relax on giant red cushions... The lighting is soft and low, enhanced by candlelight from beautiful silver candelabras...

Set the tables with floating elevated silver cherubs, below use a series of small tea-lights in silver holders. Pink slip cloths and red main cloths set the colour, consider small tables and scatter silver hearts around the setting. Have a series of cupid scenes, add gilt frames with live statues carrying golden bows. Create a romantic seating area, low tables lit in pink with a cupid projection moving gently over the area, have huge cushions each with a central red heart. Dress the bar in pink fluffy fabric and the stage to match.

Style of Invitation: Large fluffy heart

Styling: Red, pink, cupid statues, hearts, roses and candelabra

Music: Harp and flute

Drinks: Aphrodisiac cocktails, pink Champagne

Performance: Fortune teller, aura reader, cherub meet and greet

Vikings

Take a trip back in time to a very different world where the Vikings ruled the seas... Grab a shield, put on a horned helmet and join them on voyages in their famous long boats as they head for distant shores to plunder and pillage the monasteries... Join in the rowdy celebrations as the whole village gives thanks to gods such as Thor and Odin and drink and eat more than their fill long into the night...

Gorgeous muscular Vikings greet the guests, the tables are set in long lines each with a figurehead at the end and a sail set in the centre. Hessian-clad cloths run their lengths. The centre run is strewn with hurricane lamps and treasure chests filled with religious artefacts. Around the room are shields and axes alongside huge Runes with Viking symbols and flaming torches. The staff are dressed in horned helmets and leather waistcoats, the food is served on silver plates and wine from goblets.

Style of Invitation: Set of runes

Styling: Flaming torches, runes, shields, pewter religious icons, and a long boat

Music: Norwegian traditional

Drinks: Ales and wines

Performance: Fire-eaters, stunt action Vikings

Western

Yee-haw! Strap on your gun and your spurs, put on your cowboy hat and saddle up for a ride into the Wild, Wild West... The streets are dusty and tumble weed rolls by the store fronts where cowboys sit dozing under their stetsons... Hit the saloon bar and see the dancing girls, or play a hand of poker but watch out for trouble from the local cattle rustlers or the sheriff could throw you in jail for the night...

Set up an Indian reservation with tepees, with large cow-hides strung out on poles and full-size horses. Have a Western-style saloon, and make sure the bar has a flat surface to roll shots along, while beautiful saloon girls offer tequila shots to crooked gamblers that are cheating at poker. Dress the room with western store-fronts. Dance the night away to the western band and ride the bucking bronco till you fall off, and wander over to the rifle range, which is set in the jail, or have your portrait painted by the local sheriff.

Style of Invitation: Wanted poster

Styling: Corral fencing, cacti, saloon doors, tepees, horses and hay bales

Music: Western call band, blue grass

Drinks: Tequila, Bourbon, and Silver Bullet cocktails

Performance: Saloon girls, bucking bronco and cowboys for games

Wimbledon

Game, set and match... It's that time of year again, when the country prays for sunshine and all eyes turn to the courts of Wimbledon... Take a seat at centre court to enjoy all the action... Keep an eye on the scoreboard and listen to the umpire sat on high, keeping a close eye on the players... For a break from the game take a trip to the strawberry stall tempting passers-by with delicious strawberries and cream... If you fancy your chances pick up a racket and have a go yourself!

Lay the floor with astro turf and set out a court. Use stadium backdrops around the room. Serve strawberries and cream from a red and white-striped stall and champagne from another. Offer canapés on tennis rackets. Dress the tables with green cloths, use trophies for decoration. Huge oversized scoreboards tell of past victorious winners and a statue of McEnroe says it all. Catering staff are all dressed in tennis outfits.

Invites: Centre court ticket

Styling: Astro turf, nets, trophies, tennis ball pyramids, strawberry stall

Music: Jazz with summer tunes

Drinks: Pimms, Strawberry Daiquiris

Performance: Ball boys and girls and tennis jugglers, commentator

Winter Wonderland

Enter this cavern of Christmas delights and shiver with anticipation of what lies within... Here animals of the arctic make their home, penguins and polar bears nestle in the snow swept landscape amongst glistening white birch trees... Mistletoe hangs above, inviting kisses, and happy snowmen listen as sleigh bells sound in the crisp winter air....

The entrance is dressed with a stunning silver sleigh and wonderful leaping fauns. The room is an ice cave, UV lights bring alive the icebergs, the stage is covered by a snow net entwined with twinkling fairy lights. Various areas have fabulous displays of polar bears and penguins amongst icicles on soft white snowdrifts. Each table is white with iridescent snow scattered around a windswept silver twig tree and reflected on a mirrored base. Ballet dancers swirl around doing excerpts from the Nutcracker suite.

Invites: Snow shaker

Styling: Wintery whites and blues, polar bears, snowmen, penguins and sleigh

Music: String quartet and Christmas tunes

Drinks: Egg Nog and mulled wine, snowballs

Performance: Angelic ballet dancers and meet and greet nutcracker soldiers

A Rhino, a Beatle, and the Reed of the Moon

Once upon a time there was a beautiful rhino that desperately wanted to find its partner.

This rhino, so the story goes had had a most interesting, exciting and unusual life. Purchased at the auction house of Thimbleby and Shorland in October 1997 and known as the Las Vegas Rhino, he spent many years greeting clients at Theme Traders. Many recognised him and mentioned that they used to see him standing alone on a misty morning outside Oliver Reeds house, as they drove by.

Having attended many fabulous functions, under his new ownership at Theme Traders, alongside other fellow friends from the wildlife fraternity, in all sorts of venues, usually clad in greenery and African splendour, the time had come for his life to turn around once again. His birth was not clear, but rumour has it that it belonged to Ringo Starr, who gave it as a gift to the brilliant drummer Keith Moon; when he went to America he had left him on the lawn of Oliver Reed's house, with a dog, and a note, asking him to look after his pets.

Oliver Reed took on this responsibility with care, however, even though the rhino had lived in such good company he had ended up in the auction house for re-housing.

One day a film maker, James, who was filming 'Now I'm The Boss' a *documentary for Living TV about Theme Traders, mentioned that he had seen The Frank Skinner Show and Ringo Starr had said that he was looking for the original partner to his Rhino...

*a true life documentary pilot about one of Theme Traders event trainees taking the place of a senior project manager and the consequences affecting the events and the company;

Celebrations

Celebrations

There are many good reasons to have great parties and celebrations, the following chapter encompasses some really serious ones.

Around the world there seem to be celebrations for many unusual occasions, some of which are extremely interesting yet bizarre in their nature.

I have added ideas for the celebrations as well as the reasons for them. However based on the historical meaning and symbolism, it would probably not be celebrated in that manner within their own arena.

There are also occasions relating to events that are celebrated and recognised more universally. Lots of them can be cross-sectioned with the idea and concept chapter which may give a different view on entertaining for the same theme, though often adding a different edge.

After careful research it seems to me that the main motivators for celebrations in the form of national days are primarily independence and religion.

Independence day is celebrated in many countries throughout the world, a huge celebration for the country. There have recently been lots of new additions which is a reflection on the changing attitude of the world, where it is no longer acceptable as for one country to be owned by another.

Religious events such as Carnival are also celebrated widely. Even though it is a religious festival it has become a huge celebration and excuse for a spectacular party all around the world.

And what about Christmas........

Argentina - National Tango Day - December 11th

Celebrations around all the Argentinian landmarks commemorate the birthday of the nation's famous son, tango singer Carlos Gardel. Carlos was a creative genius whose entire life was dedicated to Tango. He brought together many wonderful artists and created an amazing and invaluable artwork, ëlos 14 Para el Tangoí or in English Fourteen to Tango. His work was released in 1968.

This theme lends itself to dance, so why not have a soiree dance. Make sure you have a large dance floor, get in a pair of tango dancers to give displays and participation.

Have magnificent colourful floral decorations on elevated plinths on the corners of the dance floor. Encourage all your guests to come dressed in beautiful evening attire; use tall elegant palm trees around the room and a wonderful South American band.

Flag Colours and Symbols - Pale blue and white with the golden yellow 'Sun of May' central face. The origin is Inca - Viracocha is the god creator, the sun god, and depicted as a man by the Incas. Inti is the Sun and the son of Viracocha. Inti is the astronomical object, the Sun; Incas depict Inti in the shape of a disc, with a face on it, and flaming rays around it.

Specialities: Beef, Horses, and Incas

Music and Dance: Tango

Australia Day -January 26th

Australia Day, January 26th, is the largest celebration in Australia. On January 26th 1788 Captain Arthur Phillip took formal possession of the colony of New South Wales and became its first Governor. The fledging colony soon began to celebrate the anniversary of this date. Manning Clarke notes that in 1808 the "anniversary of the foundation of the colony" was observed in the traditional manner with "drinks and merriment".

The Australians have certainly shown the world, they know how to have a party. Having worked extensively with many, there is never a week that goes by that there is not a BBQ or a drinks party at their homes. Bearing that in mind, celebrating Australian style must mean Fosters and BBQs. Consider an Australian beach party, gorgeous surfers to meet and greet; huge palm trees; hats with corks for all your guests and an informal buffet from a beach shack to accompany the BBQ.

Flag Colours and Symbols - Red, white and blue with three distinct sections. Five stars, that makes up the Southern Cross constellation from the skies of the southern hemisphere. The large star represents the six states, and the union jack is as a reminder of where the settlers came from.

Specialities: BBQs, Kangaroos, Surfing, Sheep, and Beer

Music and Dance: Didgeridoo and Aboriginal Dance

Austrian National Day - October 26th

The celebration of the 26th of October, as the Austrian National Day, goes back to the start of the 2nd Republic after WWII. Though many countries have an independence day, this one marks the day that the last foreign troops from Russia, UK, US and France left Austria in 1955 after their presence there was brought on by Austria's alliances during the Second World War. After the end of the War, Austria was occupied by the Allied powers and divided into four zones. With their consent an Austrian government was elected democratically, but every legislative regulation or political action required consent from each of the allied powers. October 26th marks the day that Austria no longer had any foreign troops on their land, and therefore the first day Austria was again an independent and sovereign country.

Offer Austrian beer in steins, create a street party and use an accordionist.
Alternatively, use the majestic background of the long gone empire, rich colours
and superb classical musicians and of course the Viennese waltz.

*Flag Colours and Symbols - Two red bands and one white central band. The
white represents the only bit of tunic left, namely the belt, without blood
on, worn by the Duke Leopold at the Battle of Ptolemas in 1191.*

Specialities: Skiing, Steins, and Musicians

Music and Dance: Folk Dance, Accordion Music and Waltzing

Brazil Carnival - 5 days before Ash Wednesday

Brazil's most famous event is Carnival, which lasts for five days from the Friday to the Tuesday immediately preceding Ash Wednesday. It is celebrated all over Brazil; Rio is the most famous and wonderful spectacle for carnival in the world. In its sambÛdromo, a tiered street designed for samba parades, there are fabulous colourful costumes, vibrant dancers and huge excitement. The top samba schools each perform in their stunning creative costumes, to an audience not only from Brazil, but from around the world.

Use bright colours for your event, vibrant floral displays, balloons and huge suns on plinths; also flame lights dressed in sequined carnival fabrics. Utilise sexy salsa music and brightly costumed dancers. At a sit down meal think about huge feather displays sitting on bright sequined overlays in the centre of the table, all colour coordinated to the table cloths, and matching throughout the room.

Flag Colours and Symbols - Green with a yellow diamond, within that a central blue globe with 27 white stars, each representing a state of the federal district, arranged like the night sky over Brazil. There is a white equatorial band across the blue globe with the motto Ordem e Progresso (order and progress)

Specialities: Masks, colourful over sized Costumes, Golden Suns, and Fireworks

Music and Dance: Street Parades, Musical Floats, and Steel Bands

Brazil - Festa de Iemanj˙ - December 31st

It is traditional in Brazil to go to the beach on New Years Eve, however some are there not to celebrate the New Year but to celebrate December 31st, the Festa de Lemanj. Lemanj is the Goddess of the Water and mother of motherhood; she is considered the front mother of all the gods in the Umbanda religion. This belief emerged in 19th century Brazil, when the spiritual entities, members of Brotherhood of Ancestral Spirits, began to manifest through mediums in rituals of cults practised by Africans and Indians, combined with elements of the Catholic religion. Lemanj is offered flowers, small presents of shells and grain that are placed into little boats and put out to the sea, sometimes they are simply just thrown into the sea. This is done to please the goddess and ask favours from her for the year to come. It is also done to thank her for her previous favours.

Use a boat to serve the buffet from, have a seascape. Combine floral, aquatic, and food elements.

Flag Colours and Symbols - Green with a yellow diamond and within that, a central blue globe with 27 white stars, each star representing a state of the federal district. They are all arranged like the night sky over Brazil. There is a white equatorial band across the blue globe with the motto Ordem e Progresso (order and progress).

Specialities: Portuguese Speaking, Coffee, Rio Carnival, and Spiritualism

Music and Dance: Samba and Capoeira

Canada Day - July 1st

On June 20, 1868, a proclamation signed by the Governor General Lord Monck, asked all Her Majesty's people, in all of Canada, to join in the celebration of, the anniversary of the formation of the union of the British North America provinces in a federation, under the name of Canada, on July 1st. The July 1st holiday was established by statute in 1879, under the name Dominion Day.

Large red and white maple leaf flags around the room; perhaps a huge grizzly bear statue as a centrepiece. Mounties for meet and greet, wearing their wonderful unique Old Campaign style head wear. The outfits can also be used as general decor.

You can bring in the great outdoors. Skiing, walking, canoeing, camping, rafting. Canada can be generally, an outdoor, sports led theme, indicative of the beauty of the wild parts of the country.

Flag Colours and Symbols - Red and white vertical bands, with central red eleven-pointed maple leaf against the white band. Red and white was sanctioned as the National colours of Canada by the Royal Proclamation that granted a coat of arms to Canada in 1921.

Specialities: Grizzly Bears, Maple Syrup, Mounted Police, Beavers, and Inuit's

Music and Dance: Folk and Ballad

Denmark - Sankthansaften (St. John's Eve) - June 23rd

This is celebrated midsummer, on the eve of St. John the Baptist's Day. The Danish celebrations, which involve a bonfire with a witch puppet on top, have been celebrated since the times of the Vikings by visiting healing water sources, and by making a large bonfire to ward away evil spirits. It is the day where the medieval wise men and women would gather special herbs that they needed for the rest of the year to cure people.

Ideas for a great party would include a bonfire and firework display; maybe a series of witches around the room; this area could be set as a Viking encampment with cauldrons of faux flames. Offer traditional Danish food on upturned Viking shields, and Danish beer from ceramic jugs. Horned helmets are fun for the guests.

Flag Colours and Symbols - Red and white Scandinavian cross symbolically, white for peace and honesty, red for hardiness, bravery, strength & valour, thought to have derived from the Danish coats of arms used during the Crusades. Another possibility is that it is based on the coat of arms of Lubeck, which was red with a white cross.

Specialities: Vikings, Hans Christian Andersen Fairy Tales, and Trolls

Music and Dance: Ballet - through the courts, and Folk music

Egypt -Sham al Nessim - Monday after Coptic Easter

The first day of spring is called Sham al Nessim, meaning, "sniffing the breeze". It welcomes in the spring. Sham al Nessim coincided with the vernal equinox, and the ancients believed that this day represented the beginning of creation. The date was not fixed, it was announced every year on the evening before the feast at the foot of the Great Pyramid. The feast of 'Shamo,' means 'renewal of life' the word changed during the Coptic age to 'shamm' (smelling or breathing) and the word 'Nessim' (breeze) was added. The ancient Egyptians first celebrated the feast of Shamo in 2700 BC.

Make large sculptures from the food, shape into pyramids; this can be done with all fare such as rice, cous cous, fruit and Dates. Use palm trees and statues as decorations; create a lovely chill out area with beautiful soft fabric swags in gold and creams, and set Egyptian hangings on the walls.

Flag Colours and Symbols - Red white and black bands, with a shield imposed on a golden eagle above a scroll. The eagle of Salah ad Din, the Sultan who ruled Egypt and Syria in the 12th Century, and who is better known in the west as Saladin of the Crusades.

Specialities: Pyramids, Hieroglyphics, Camels, Dessert, and Feeseekh -salted mullet

Music and Dance: Belly Dancing, and Snake Charming with Flute

France - Bastille Day -14th July

Bastille Day, on the fourteenth of July, is the French symbol of the end of the Monarchy and the beginning of the First Republic. The people of Paris rose up and decided to march on the Bastille, a state prison that stood for the absolute despotism of the Ancient Regime. For all citizens of France, the storming of the Bastille symbolizes, liberty, democracy, and the struggle against all forms of oppression. The following year the citizens gathered to celebrate, and to this day, it is celebrated everywhere in France. On July 16, the King recognized the tricolour, the red white and blue cockade: the Revolution had succeeded.

Certainly use flags; have an area representing the richness of the monarchy, use fabulous gold cutlery and an Eiffel Tower on the table; have views, from a beautiful chateaux out to lovely manicured gardens; create a reception area - the Bastille, a rough floor, with upturned barrels, drinks from earthenware goblets, and musty prison guards to entertain the guests as they enter.

Flag Colours and Symbols: Red, white and blue vertical equal spaced stripes. The colours were originally believed to originate from the naval flag. The origins of the 'tricolore' are said to be from a rosette, created in July 1789, during the French Revolution. It used the colours of the coat of arms of Paris (red and blue) and the royal colour (white). The flags kept changing after that, but then ended up reverting to the original concept, the 'tricolore'.

Specialities: Mussels, Frogs Legs, Champagne, Camargue Horses, and the Eiffel Tower

Music and Dance: Moulin Rouge, Can Can, and Accordion

Germany - Oktoberfest - Sept - Oct

The October Festival originated nearly two hundred years ago. Racing horses and many other gaily decorated entertainments were used to celebrate the wedding of the Crown Prince, who later became King Ludwig I of Bavaria, and married Princess Therese von Sachsen-Hildburghausen on the 17th October 1810. It is a sixteen-day festival beginning with the mayor of Munich having the first sip of beer. It has become a celebration, and highly visual event; the entertainments still continue offering an opportunity for the show of traditional costume; lots of Weiss beer and entertainment.

Long tables laid out with the blue and white triangular flags from Bavaria. Local Sausages and Sauerkraut, both of which are the perfect accompaniments to the traditional white beers served in Steins. Entertainment should include an Oompah band, certainly with an accordionist. Use lederhosen for the catering staff and perhaps have a beer tasting opportunity.

Flag Colours and Symbols - Black, red and gold, the old colours of the 1848 revolution and the Weimar democracy. A speaker in the Parliamentary Council put it this way: "The tradition of black, red and gold is unity in freedom." It is believed the colours represented the uniforms of the students who fought the Napoleonic occupation of much of Germany. Another story suggests that the colours are derived from the black eagle on gold, on the Imperial coat of arms of the Holy Roman Empire.

Specialities: Beer, Lederhosen, Weiss Bier, Sauerkraut, and Alpine Bell Ringing

Music and Dance: Schulplattler - toe-slappinp, Oompah band,

Greece - Apokries - 3 weeks before lent

It is particularly interesting how Apokries is celebrated in Greece. In ancient times Dionysis, the God of wine and food was worshipped, yet the Apokries means the giving up of meat, which is also is the same as the Latin words carne, and vale, i.e. carnival, is 'goodbye to meat.' The Greeks hold parties and celebrations throughout the period, however, in the last week they really party, very much non-stop. They also spend most of their time in tavernas, and in high spirits with their friends. In many countries, the last day before Lent has a different name, it is called Mardi Gras, Shrove Tuesday, Carnival, or Fasching and has become a last date to celebrate before Lent.

Serve mezzes and Ouzo; decorate the room with a fisherman's boat, lobster pots and traditional rural artefacts; use beautiful olive trees in pots mixed with lemon trees, and don't forget the old Greek tradition of breaking plates, and participating with the fabulous Greek dancing.

Flag Colours and Symbols: Light blue and white. The colour scheme of blue and white was first used in the 1820s and represents the colours of the famous Greek sky, sea, white clouds and waves. It is based on nine equal horizontal stripes of blue alternating with white. The white cross symbolises Greek Orthodoxy, and the nine stripes are thought to represent the nine syllables of the phrase " E-lef-the-ri-a i Tha-na-tos" which means "Freedom or Death" though many believe, they symbolise the nine Muses, the goddesses of art and civilisation

Specialities: Calamari, Ouzo, Greek Mythology, Statues and Columns, Plate Smashing

Music and Dance: Homer, Lutes, and Greek Dancing

Holland - Queen's Birthday - April

Dutch people celebrate the Queen's Birthday on April 30th as a national holiday, although it is actually the birth date of the former queen, Juliana. Her daughter Beatrix became queen in a ceremony on April 30th, 1980. The Dutch put up the national flag, they bring out the royal pennant and try to turn everything in Holland into a sea of orange. They face paint everyone orange, and also decorate their cars, and even paint their bicycles orange. This is all to celebrate the official birthday of Her Majesty, the Queen of Orange. Orange was actually a principality and not anything to do with the colour.

Edam rolling is a popular game to get your guests going. Dress the room with beautiful flowers in whitewashed barrows; use vases full of oranges; arrange seat covers in orange, and dress the stage with orange drapes and a windmill. Serve canapés from clogs, and old Genevre as an aperitif.

Flag Colours and Symbols: Red: white and blue currently, though it changed from orange, white, and blue, taken from the coat of arms of the Prince of Orange; a rebel, who was head of a band of revolutionaries, called The Watergeuzen (pro-independence pirates). Acting for him, they harassed the enemy everywhere they could; they did this under a tricolour. After several more changes to the flag, it was reverted back, and then because it was seen to be to dull, the red replaced the Orange.

Specialities, Edam Cheese, Clogs, Bicycles, Canals, Windmill Cookies, Flowers and Tulips

Music and Dance: Clog dancing, and Abba

India - Diwali - November

The happiest and most colourful festival of the Hindu calendar is celebrated extensively in November. Fireworks are always used in this colourful celebration of the gods. Diwali means the festival of lights, which is why both fireworks and firecrackers play such an important part in the best known of Hindu celebrations, and certainly the brightest. Light Amidst the darkest skies, is the sign of welcome to the gods Rama and Lakshmi. Families get together and celebrate with sweetmeats, gifts and massive feasts. Most families will decorate their homes with flowers and create a colourful, intricate detailed pattern made in rice flour, this is called a rangoli, and is positioned at the entrance of their home.

Beautiful coloured saris for dressings, wonderful Indian elephants totally jewelled, Indian lanterns, Taj Mahal paintings, statues of Ganeesh and other Gods. Bindis, for all the guests.

Flag Colours and Symbols: Three bands, saffron, white in the middle and then a green band. The centre of the white band has a navy blue wheel with 24 spokes, known as the Chakra (energy point) or the Ashoka Chakra. Ashoka was an emperor in 273bc who was also a convert to Buddhism. The flag is known as Tiranga or tricolour, but normally a tricolour has no symbols. The Chakra symbol was taken from the Ashok pillar at Sarnath

Specialities: Curries, Bollywood, Saris, Indian sweets and Indian Gods

Music and Dance: Indian Bands with Cymbals and *Indian Dancing
*Often performed with palm-upraised gestures,
an expression of protection and reassurance.

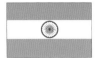

Ireland - St. Patrick's Day

Saint Patrick was the patron saint and national apostle of Ireland. He had landed there after a kidnapping and was sent to Ireland as a slave, around AD 390. He was famous for two works, one a spiritual biography and the other a damning of the British mistreatment of Irish Christians. He is well known also for driving snakes from Ireland, though Ireland is not believed to have had snakes! So perhaps it was the snake symbols worshipped by pagans.

St. Patrick's day is always celebrated in a party like fashion throughout the world. Large shamrocks and Guinness are a traditional way to set the scene, though a wonderful woodland setting with small leprechauns and mushrooms afloat with little fairies is quite magical.

Flag Colours and Symbols: Tricolour of green, white and orange. Originally the green represented the Catholic Gaelic community, the Protestant community was represented in Orange, due to William of Orange, and the white was for the peace; symbolic of the fact that both communities were living together in harmony.

Specialities: Guinness, Potatoes, Gypsy and Fortune Tellers

Music and Dance: Danny Boy and Molly Malone Tunes, Irish fiddlers, and Traditional Dance - River Dance

Jamaica - Junkonoo - December 26th & January 1st

I added this, as it is a fun and bizarre twist on a traditional Christmas party. Jamaican's celebrate Christmas by putting on scary costumes and dancing around the streets, they call it Junkonoo. A carnival day, with music, stunning costumes, singing and street parties. The origins of Junkanoo vary. Though originated in the Bahamas, the most accepted thought is that the word "Junkanoo" comes from the name John Canoe, who was an African prince and slave trader operating on the Gold Coast in the 17th century. He was said to have outwitted the English therefore, the Dutch and English alike feared him. To the slaves however, he was a hero and was worshipped and idolized by all of them.

A Caribbean setting with street shacks dressed with old car tyres, amongst bamboo and reeds. Reggae, whether a band or recorded music is a must. Huge sun images could dress the stage; never forget the rum cocktails served from coconut shells.

Flag Colours and Symbols: Green, black and gold. Green is symbolic for the future and land, gold is for the sun and natural wealth, and black for the people, their creativity and strength.

Specialities: Rum, exotic Rum Cocktails and Beach Parties

Music and Dance: Reggae, Bob Marley, Steel Drums and Calypso

214

Japan-Tanabata Matsuri (Star Festival) - July 7th

Tanabata, also known as the "star festival", takes place on the 7th day of the 7th month of every year. It is a romantic legend that stars Altair and Vega, which are normally separated from each other, like unaccepted lovers, by the Milky Way, are able to meet. Custom has that you write your wish on a piece of paper, and hang that piece of paper on a specially erected bamboo tree, the decorated bamboo branch is tied to a pole and placed in front of the house in the hope that the wishes become true.

Use beautiful cherry blossom for decorating the tables. If possible have a geisha girl to meet and greet, use bamboo cups and to give the room a magical feel, put tall bamboo in large golden pots near golden cranes all against a tranquil night garden setting. Place a large Buddha as a focal piece, set with small brass pots of spices and candles around it. Consider hanging colourful lanterns by the dance floor, and silhouettes of a Japanese temple all add to the ambience

Flag Colours and Symbols: A large red central disc, representing the sun, is set on a white background. The sun symbol has been used in Japanese art, such as fans and paintings since the twelfth century, it is believed to be symbolically related. It is affectionately known as Hinomaru that literally means sun disc.

Specialities: Sushi, Tatami, Saki, Bamboo, Kimono, Fans

Music and Dance: Karaoke, Kabuki - Japanese theatre, Taiko Drums

Kazakhstan - New Year - 22 March

This date is a New Year's Eve according to the ancient Oriental calendar. It celebrates the vernal equinox, the first day of spring. It is also known as "Ulys Kuni" (The first day of the New Year) or "Ulystyn uly kuni" (The great day of the people).

As the country is so multi-cultural you can consider the use of traditional items, and also elements from the different cultures that make up this country. Perhaps, oversized Russian dolls and fabulous backdrops of the vast snowy landscapes, bring them together with a series of stunning images of nomads and their large hanging carpets, for which they are so famous. Add a huge rocket and a blue star cloth as a focal point as much of the country has been used for rocket experiments.

Flag Colours and Symbols: Sky blue and gold symbols. The blue represents the various Turkic people making today's population. It is symbolic as it represents the sky god Gok-Gök-Tanry, "the eternal wide blue sky"; another interpretation is that the blue background stands for the sky, and for freedom. The golden eagle is associated with the empire of Genghis Khan, who ruled under a blue banner with such an eagle on it, in Kazakhstan. The side pattern represents the old culture and traditions.

Specialities: Nomads, Rockets, Bright Carpets, Healers and Mystics

Music and Dance: Bards and Singing Storytellers

Kenya - Jamhuri Day - December 12th

Jamhuri Day is an Independence day celebration; during Jamhuri Day there is an overwhelming theme of unity, which does not change as they feast, dance and, parade. The speeches are all representative of being in unity with each other. With so much socialising going on the Kenyans keep a close focus on this unity, which is one of the most important values of their culture. Jamhuri Day is a huge celebration where people get together not only for eating and drinking, but also for dance and music.

Use huge tusks for the entrance, lay the table with faux skins, and use a drum as a centrepiece. Have African music and colourful African dress for the catering staff. Try serving some traditional African dishes such as Ugali, which is made up of ground maize flour and water. It is like small cakes after it has been cooked

Flag Colours and Symbols: Black, red and green split by thin white stripes, with a central Masaii shield and spears motif. Black represents the people; red represents blood and the struggle for freedom; green represents Kenya's agriculture and natural resources; white represents togetherness and peace. The shield and spears motif in black, red and white symbolizes the defence of freedom and the struggle for independence.

Specialities: Wood Carving, Spears, Shields, Animals, Vivid Coloured Clothing, Wooden Beads, and Ground Nut Soup served from Calabash Bowls, (dried shell from the fruit tree)

Music and Dance: Tribal Dance and Drums

Luxembourg - Brgsonndeg (Bonfire Day) - February 28th

Celebrates the end of winter and symbolises the victory of the sun over winter. Young people climb a nearby hill and build a great bonfire to mark the changing of the seasons. It is said that it may be symbolic of the last burning of witches by the Inquisition. Starting the fire is seen as an honour and generally is given to the last couple married.

Burning the Buerg - as it is called, consists of burning a large pile of straw, brushwood and logs.

Have a bonfire night party, huge flames, warm toddies, and not forgetting fireworks, Dried floral arrangements and huge symbolic sun statues.

Flag Colours and Symbols: Red white and blue horizontal stripes, colours believed to have been taken from the medieval coat of arms of the Grand Duke of Luxembourg. Part of the beautiful design is a golden lion on a central blue and white striped shield. The flag is also the same as the Dutch flag apart from the variation in colours.

Specialities: Wine, potatoes, Bonfirese, The Grand Duke and a Fairground

Music and Dance: Fiddler, Folk Music and Classical Music

Mexico - Dia de los Muertos - November 2nd

A rather back to front celebration that has turned from a sad occasion to one in which you are inviting the dead home; they are supposed to return on this day, and furthermore you should celebrate their return. Dìa de los Muertos is held the day after All Saints' Day on November 2nd.

The theme is certainly festive, even though many families will still set a small alter dressed with bright flowers and small colourful gifts, somewhere in their homes, for their friends and families.

Food should be traditional Mexican, try making skulls from sugar and check out
the recipe for "pan de muerto," otherwise known as bread of the dead.

Flag Colours and Symbols: Green white and red vertical stripes with a central coat of arms believed to be based on an old legend where the Aztecs were guided by Huitzilopochtli to seek a place where an eagle landed on a prickly-pear cactus, eating a snake. After hundreds of years of searching they found this sign on a small swampy island in Lake Texcoco. They named Mexico-Tenochtitlan meaning, "In the Moon's navel-Place of the Prickly Pear Cactus". In AD1325 they built a city on the site of the island in the lake; this is now the centre of Mexico City.

Specialities: Sombreros, Skulls, Skeletons, Ponchos, Tortillas and Cactii

Music and Dance: Mariachi Band and Ranchero Music (Mexican Cowboy Music)

Nepal - Dasain - September - October

An auspicious occasion. It consists of two weeks of feasts and celebrations. The celebration commemorates a great victory of the gods over the wicked demons. The main celebration glorifies the success of good over evil and is symbolized by the goddess Durga slaying the terrible demon Mahisasur, who terrorised the earth in the disguise of a brutal water buffalo.

A series of colourful god statues, beautiful flower garlands to greet the guests, and not forgetting the huge sacred cow dressed with beautiful bells and colourful attire. Centralise a large Buddha as a focal piece, set with small brass pots of spices and candlelight's. Use red white and blue for table decorations, to reflect the beautiful Nepalese flag, consider hanging these by the dance floor. Colourful lanterns and silhouettes of a Nepalese temple all add to the ambience.

Flag colours and Symbols: Red and blue with white symbols; it represents different branches of the previous rulers, the Rana dynasty. It consists of two pennants joined in the middle. The blue border means peace and the red colour is Nepal's national colour. The two royal symbols are now declared to represent the hope that Nepal will last as long as the moon and the sun.

Specialities: Temples, Festivals, Buddhas, Himalayas, Jungle and Mount Everest

Music and Dance: Buddhist Chants, Bell Ringing, Gongs and Drumming

Norway - Tyvendedgen - January 13th

This is celebrated always the twentieth day after Christmas.

Saint Knut drives Christmas away. The story goes that Kari Tretten the troll woman led sleighs across mystical frozen lakes and down frosty roads jingling bells as they went. Traditionally Norwegians chop up their Christmas trees and pop them in the bonfire as this is the last day to have a Christmas party, and so it is celebrated with friends and in traditional style.

For styling add a few trolls and Snow covered fir trees around the room. Have a roaring fire and set a beautiful Mountain backdrop as a background. Do not forget the tree decorations, but replace them with chocolate ones for your guests to eat before the ritual tree burning.

Flag Colours and Symbols: Red background with blue and white cross, similar design to Swedish flags as they were originally flown as one.

Specialities: Vikings, Fjords, Pickled Herrings and Fish Cakes called Kristiansundball

Music and Dance: Hardanger Fiddle, Folk Dancing, Sami Music with Runebomme - meaning the Shaman's Drum

Oman - Eid al-Fitr

As Oman is mainly Muslim and there are not many other interesting celebrations for the letter O,
seemed appropriate to allocate it to one of the most celebrated events of the Muslim lunar calenda
the end of Ramadan. Ramadan is a fast that lasts from daybreak to sunset and is meant as a time
consider people less fortunate than yourself and be grateful for your blessings.

Traditional Arabic feasts would lend themselves to exotic areas clad with palm
trees, each table should be set with brocade runners and the room lit by huge
beautiful lanterns. Use star cloths to represent the magnificent Arabian nights
and put a camel at the entrance, resting under the shade of a palm tree.

Flag Colours and Symbols: Red green and white stripes against a vertical red strip, the
national emblem of crossed swords and a centred a silver double sided dagger from
Oman, called a Khanjar is placed on the upper left corner. The white represents the
Imam (religious leaders) and peace and prosperity, the green is for Islam, and the fertility
of the country, its northern Green Mountains, and the red it is said to represent battles
against foreign invaders. It is also the colour of the flag of the Al Bu Said dynasty.

Specialities: Frankincense Trees, Dates, Coffee with Cardamom Seeds, Henna and Soukhs

Music and Dance: The Razha Dance - performed by men, with Sword Dancing
and displays of strength. Drums, Flute, Lute and Belly Dancing

Portugal - June 10 - Portugal Day

This is also called National Day; it is a particularly interesting event which is dedicated to the arts. It marks the death of Luis de Camoes who wrote an epic poem called Os Lusiadas (1572) after Portugal's people and the work chronicled the voyages of Vasco de Gama, before a huge array of strangely mixed Christian and Pagan images.

A Medieval style should be adopted, suitable for lords, ladies, and royalty with wrought iron candelabras, riches and treasures. Paintings of famous seafarers, and an elegantly laid long table set with golden cutlery. Style an entrance with a huge ships wheel and hanging lanterns. Thrones for the hosts, and velvet clad benches or high-backed chairs for the guests.

Flag Colours and Symbols: Red representing bloodshed and courage in revolutionary combat, the green part for hope. The golden circle is a navigational instrument called an armillary sphere, it represents new lands found in fifteenth/sixteenth centuries, where the Portuguese set up trading and it's one time colonial empire founded by, Prince Henry the Navigator. The blue shields represent the five Moorish Kings defeated by the king of Portugal Alfonso Henriques 1. The white dots, religious cross design represent the five nails used on Christ, and the seven castles are the conquest castles from the Moors.

Specialities: Sardines, Port wine, Pasteis de Nata (custard tarts) Bullfights and Sweet Figs

Music and Dance: Folk Music, Folk Dancing, Fado Singing and Guitar

Qatar - Muharram

Muharram sets the beginning of the first month in the Islamic calendar. It is the Muslim New Year. It remembers the day in 622 AD on which Mohammed and his followers left Mecca for Medina; it was an event that then and now is now considered the start of Islamic history. His flight is called Hegira. The celebration for this is very different from other celebrations, invites go out to friends to visit and get together. When they meet they talk mainly about the beginning of Islam and then recount many stories related to it. Sometimes they beat their hands on their chests to demonstrate their point.

Use gazebos dressed as beautiful Bedouin style tents set up with low tables and huge hookah pipes; serve fun desserts with exotic names such as Umm Ali (meaning "Mother of Ali"), a bread pudding or a sweet cheesecake with a cream topping, known as Esh Saraya, "bread of the harem."

Flag Colours and Symbols: A maroon base with a nine-pointed white serrated stripe on the left side of it. The white represents peace and the serration represents Qatar as the 9th member of the 'reconciled Emirates' of the Arabian Gulf at the conclusion of the Qatari-British treaty in 1916. The maroon, which was formerly red, and it is said, to be what becomes of red, as it fades in the Gulf sun, represents the Kharijite Muslims who populate the region and the blood spilt in Qatar's wars.

Specialities: Arabian White Oryx, Weaving, Rugs, Cushions and Tents, Falconry, Pearls and Gold

*Music and Dance: Story Telling, Dancing with Veils, and Az-Zaffan -
This consists of individual dances accompanied by popular songs, jumping
in the air, swaying to lute and mirwas small goat skin drums*

Russia - Maslyanitsa (Pancake Week) - March 2-9th

The last week before lent the Russians celebrate with pancakes in a pagan celebration, Cult of the Suní. The theme is to say goodbye to the icy winter and welcome to the brighter spring. Ancient Slavs believed that rituals and ceremonies could help make the Sun bring its warmth to the Earth and speed up the arrival of spring. The traditional way to bring on the sun is to party, celebrate, and drive around in Troikas. The culmination of this holiday involves burning a winter scarecrow. Before lent begins, Russian people welcome guests, and bake pancakes which symbolize the Sun, they also enjoy medovukhaî, a traditional Russian drink made of honey. Maslyanitsa - means "butter" in Russian.

Style the event with bright yellow and golds, use a scarecrow as a centrepiece surrounded by wintery twig trees. Bunches of spring flowers and oversized Russian dolls look great.

Flag colours and symbols: A tricolour consisting of three equal horizontal stripes, all with special Russian symbolic meanings, the white on top for nobility, freedom, and sincerity, the blue stands for truthfulness, honour, commitment and purity, and is also considered the colour of the Mother of God, Patroness of Russian ground, the red symbolises love, courage, and valour. This was the original Imperial Flag flown on early Russian shipping vessels more than 300 years ago. The colour of the stripes later also symbolized the unity of the three Eastern Slavic Nations - Byelorussia, Ukraine and Russia.

Specialities: Matryoshka (nesting dolls) Tea Ceremony with a Samovar, and Cossacks.

Music and Dance: Cossack Dancing, Gypsy Music and Ballet

Spain-Dia del Hispanidad (Columbus Day) - October 12th

Christopher Columbus had set sail in a westerly direction with three ships the Niña, the Pinta and the Santa Maria, to explore and conquer new lands for Spain. A sailor on board one of the ships, the Pinta, sighted land early in the morning of October 12th 1492 and this lead to the celebration. The following day, they landed on the Bahamian island of Guanahanì, ending a voyage that had begun nearly ten weeks earlier in Palos, Spain.

This can be a traditional Spanish affair with Tapas and Sangria; colourful posters and flamenco dancers and a Spanish guitarist; castanets are nice for your guests to play. Create a tapas bar and have the food laid out on a buffet, alternativel, set the table with maps on scrolls and use oil filled hurricane lamps for light. Go back in time, have sailors to serve the drinks and food; a huge globe as a focal point; a Christopher Columbus, character to meet, greet and tell tales of the furthest shores. Ships wheels, old ship's sails and flags look great around a room.

Flag Colours and Symbols: This flag has a lot of controversy surrounding the meaning of its colours, there is a large yellow band running horizontally across its belly, above and below are bands in red, the civil flag does not have the coat of arms on and the military flag does. Every year there is a ceremony where the military swear allegiance to the flag, the commoners are also allowed to participate if arranged in advance, this is called 'The jura de bandera' (flag oath). The flag colours it is said, were chosen in a competition, yet others argue they are based on the heraldic pennants of the Spanish kingdoms. Another possibility is that it was the Naples flag adopted by Carlos III.

Specialities: Bull fighting, Tapas, Beaches, Gazpacho and Cava

Music and Dance: Spanish Guitar and Flamenco

Thailand - Songkran Day - 13th-15th April

The word Songkran is from the Sanskrit meaning the beginning of a new Solar Year - the traditional Thai New Year the date varies with the lunar calendar. It is believed that the mythical serpent, Nagas brought on rain by spouting water from the sea. Water throwing has become a large part of the celebration, along with the release of beautiful birds and fish. The origins of this came from the days when the farmers would collect last remaining fish from dried up waters and keep them till the waters came again to release them to stock the rivers and canals. Sonkrant also has religious aspects related to the memory of the dead. Bones of the dead can even be brought to the Wat for blessings, young people wash the hands of the elders with scented waters to gain respect. Buddhas are cleaned and washed and monks given copious amounts of food.

Water fountains, beautiful orchids, pagodas and temples. Buddha's, and colourful Thai umbrellas. Bring your guests in with a monk striking a gong. Serve canapès from fish shaped platters.

Flag Colours and Symbols: Thai actually means the word free. This flag has five horizontal stripes red, white, blue, white and red. The colours mean red for nation, white for religion and blue for the king. The motto for Thailand though deemed unofficial, is Nation- Religion-King. One story mentions that during a flood, King Vajiravudh (Rama VI) saw the flag hanging upside-down and so this could not happen again he created a new symmetrical flag. In 1917 the middle colour was changed to blue, the colour representing Friday, the day he was born. It is also said that the blue was chosen to show solidarity with the Allies of World War I, which contained the same colours in their flags.

Specialities: Green Curry, Buddha's, Temples, Floating Markets and Monks

Music and Dance: Thai Dancing, Kick Boxing. Gongs and Finger Cymbals

United States of America - Groundhog Day - February 2nd

Groundhog Day, February 2nd, is a popular tradition in the United States. Germany has a similar belief about a hedgehog on the same day.

It is a legend that has been passed down many centuries. Its origins related to animals and ethnic culture, perhaps it is all relating back to nature and how we would use these signs significantly. It is the day that the Groundhog comes out of his hole after a long winter sleep to look for his shadow, if he sees the shadow it means six more weeks of winter, if not, hey spring is on its way!

Elevate statues of groundhogs onto columns decorated with stars and stripes
and rotate them. Dress the table in sparkling fabric in red white and blue; add
matching chair covers and set in front of a magical wintery backdrop.

Flag Colours and Symbols: It has thirteen horizontal stripes representing its original thirteen colonies. The stripes start red alternating with white and finishing with red. The left hand corner has a blue rectangle with fifty small, white, five-pointed pentagram stars representing the states, all arranged in nine rows. Pentagrams are not, simply a five-pointed star: the symbol must be composed of five lines, it must include the interior pentagon. The pentagram has long been associated with the planet Venus as it seems when viewed from Earth, the planet Venus plots a near perfect pentagram shape around the Sun every eight years, returning to its exact starting point after a forty year cycle.

Specialities: Hot dogs, Baseball, Yellow Taxis, Las Vegas, and Neon's

 *Music and Dance: Cheerleaders, Marching Bands, Elvis and Liberace*

Vatican - Christmas - December 25th

The Vatican, as the recognised holy Catholic city, is one of the many places to allocate Christmas. The celebration of the birth of Christ. The traditional Christmas feast, with friends and family. Many joyful decorations and customs had very little to do with Christmas, for interest I have added a few details.

Father Christmas- Alias Kriss Kringle and Saint Nicholas was really a 4th century bishop. He held a feast directed at children on 6th December. The English started celebrating the feast day on Christmas 25th December.

Mistletoe - Druids believed that mistletoe fell from the heavens and onto a tree from earth, therefore a kiss underneath the mistletoe can be quite romantic as well as meaning a join up of heaven and earth.

Flag colours and symbols: The flag of the Vatican City consists of two bands of yellow and white. The symbol consists of two crossed keys, silver and gold to represent the keys of Saint Peter. It is said that he had the keys to the kingdom of heaven. There is also the Miter or crown, of the pope.

Christmas trees - Offered as a symbol of Christianity. It started when St. Boniface cut down Thor's Oak at Geismar. The tree was central to a Germanic tribes pagan beliefs and it was their place of worship to the god of thunder. A new fir tree grew and St. Boniface converted the heathens to Christianity. They then started decorating the tree for Christmas.

Specialities: Swiss guards, (mercenaries) Christmas Trees, Religious Artefacts and the Pope

Music and Dance: Carol Singing, Christmas Mass and Sacred Music

Wales - St. David's Day - March 1st

St David's Day (St. David was known as Dewi Sant) is now the traditional day of Wales and celebrated by Welsh people all over the world. St David's Day has been a national festival in Wales since the 18th century. His mother was also a Saint called St.Non, so was his teacher. It was said he was having a sermon on a hill and the earth elevated from the ground so his attendees could hear him better. The celebration usually consists of singing and eating and gatherings of friends include a tea with the rendition of traditional songs. The mythical red dragon is flown as a flag or worn as a pin, brooch or pendant also daffodils and leeks are worn, and leeks sometimes eaten. One legend tells of a battle between the Welsh and the Saxons fought in a field of leeks.

Use the colours of Wales, green red and white, offer your guests a buttonhole daffodil as they arrive serve miniature cups of leek and potatoes soup, book a wonderful Welsh singer..Tom Jones

Flag Colours and symbols: The flag of Wales is the mythical Red Dragon standing on a green field with a white background, the colours of the Royal Tudors royal badge, or perhaps it simply represents the leek. The dragon is accepted in varying guises on the flag. The union jack represents Wales on it with the St. George's Cross, most peculiar, as there is no St. David's Cross. Wales supposedly is represented by default when England became the kingdom of England and Wales; another possibility is that the flag represents the three united kingdoms, which are the kingdoms of England, Scotland and Ireland. Wales is not a kingdom, it's a principality and therefore it is not represented.

Specialities: Daffodils, Dragons and Myths, Mining, Leeks and Rugby

Music and Dance: Tom Jones, Charlotte Church and 'Cerdd Dant' with Harp

Zambia - N'cwala -February 24th

The Zambians are honouring the day in 1835 when the Ngoni, a tribe from the Eastern Province, first crossed the Zambezi River. The celebration of this success is now combined with a first harvest festival. At the N'cwala, which actually means the First Fruits ceremony, the Ngoni people perform dances in a warrior style and then slaughter a black bull. The villagers feast on beef stew and corn. When the chief has tasted the first produce of the year and drunk the blood from the bull, the harvest begins. Warrior Dancing is predominant and a series of twelve tribal chieftains are guests accompanied by their best dancers in full tribal attire, accessorised by fabulous animal headdresses, to compete for the respectful title of best dancers given by the chief.

Zambian art is amazing; hand carved animal figures, long necked Giraffes as centrepieces, stylised antelopes painted in tribal colours. Spears and shields and colourful tribal costumes.

Flag colours and symbols: The green background is for the land of Zambia and the importance of agriculture and all nature in the land. The red bar symbolizes the struggle for freedom, the black bar for the people of Zambia, and the copper bar for natural resources and mineral wealth. The fish eagle is the national bird, and represents the people's ability to rise above the nation's problems

Specialities: Chibuku Shake Shake, (sorghum and maize brew), Nshima (maize balls) Victoria Waterfalls, Wildlife, Hand Carved Canoes, Traditional Healers, Livingstone (Memorial)

Music and Dance: Drumming, Traditional and Ceremonial African Dancing, Whistles and Thumb Pianos - made with gourds

POD...for children

This year Pod entertainers will provide over 1800 shows in hospitals all over Britain, on wards or at bedsides making around 20,000 children feel better.

£50 will fund one Pod show - £600 will fund 12 monthly shows

No one likes being in hospital, least of all children. Treatment is necessary, but children are frightened and parents feel worried. Often children suffer acute pain. Hospitals increasingly try to make a child's stay in hospital as pleasant as possible. But hospitals have limited funding for non-essential, non-medical activities·

Over the last 29 years, POD has helped to bring magic fun and laughter into the lives of many thousands of sick children in hospital.

POD employs specially selected professional children's entertainers, who are happy to do hospital shows for less than their usual fee. They make balloon animals or juggle, they make animals talk or things disappear, they make music or magic - and most important of all, they are sensitive to the needs of sick children. They can be silly, funny, serious or tender - it all depends on what the children need. Pod is centrally co-ordinated and works closely with hospital staff to ensure that shows are a success and children really do benefit. The power and potential of relaxation, participation, fun and laughter are increasingly appreciated. Happy children get better quicker.

Pod's ultimate aim is to provide shows at all hospitals and hospices which admit children, but shows have to be paid for, and Pod's funds are limited. All Pod's funds are spent on entertaining children in hospital. Pod's administrative costs are funded by the Pod League of Friends.

Excert from a letter from a nurse at Northampton General Hospital:

Dear Margaret,

Just a quick note to say how grateful Newcastle Genteral Hospital are for your great service.

We specialise in children who have breain tumours. Many of these children spend months in hospital, the visits from the POD entertainers are often the highlight of the children's stays. To see a child smile can often be essential therapy for that child and their family.

As the nursery nurse on the ward I fully appreciate the benefits of these visits and often use them as part of my play therapy sessions.

On behalf of all the staff, children and families, thankyou so much.

Pod can't make children better but it can make them feel better. Happy children get better faster.

Index

Acknowledgements and Many Thanks

*Catherine de Goris has kindly helped me create the layout for this book
and her creative input and thoughts are valued ...Thankyou.*

*Catherine Sterry has brought the best out of our images and as usual solved all our
'challenges' in her usual wonderful, thoughtful and creative manner ...Thankyou.*

*Thanks to all my friends at Theme Traders who helped in many many ways
to make this book possible, creating beautiful events, with pictures and super
ideas.... Especially, Natalie Kiley, Lisa Proto and Alexandra Munro.*

*Rowan Phillpot amongst others, created the lovely story boards,
many thanks and keep those creative juices flowing.*

Siobhán O'Donoghue for her eagle eyes.

Maurice Godden, Molly, Sheena and Neil for their ongoing enthusiasm, help and support.

*All my contributors and celebrities, who have not only provided lovely reading and shared
wonderful memories but also are supporting Pod... for Children by participating in this book.*

*Ringo Starr for adding so much interest in our beautiful rhino. Because of his interest I came across
a rhino called Ringo, for adoption from The Sebakwe Black Rhino Trust. I adopted him from them
and hopefully he will now have a long safer life. Lots more rhinos also need to be adopted...*

Contacts

Theme Traders - www.themetraders.com - tel: +44 (0) 20 8452 8518

Pod for children - www.podcharity.org.uk - tel: 01938 810374

The Sebakwe Black Rhino Trust - www.blackrhino.org - tel: 01993 830278

Party...

written by Kim Einhorn

Designed and published
by Theme Traders Publishing.

All images are derived from original photography of Theme
Traders events and archives. All rights reserved. No reproduction,
in any form, copy or transmission of this publication, including
photography may be made without written permission.

copyright © Kim Einhorn

Theme Traders
The Stadium
Oaklands Road
London
NW2 6DL

t. +44 (0) 20 8452 8518
f. +44 (0) 20 8450 7322
e. mailroom@themetraders.com
www.themetraders.com

Front cover design and photograph by Kim Einhorn

Printed by Butler & Tanner

Limited Edition

ISBN 0-9542453-1-8   ISBN 978-0-9542453-1-3